LEGENDARY CANADIAN WOMEN

LEGENDARY
CANADIAN
WOMEN

by
Carol McLeod

Lancelot Press,
Hantsport, N.S.

To Auntie May who believed:
"To patient faith the prize is sure"
this book is lovingly dedicated.

ISBN 0-88999-215-0

Published 1983

LANCELOT PRESS LIMITED, Hantsport, N.S.
Office and plant situated on Highway No. 1, ½ mile east of Hantsport

ACKNOWLEDGMENTS

My thanks are due to the interlibrary loan coordinator of the Moncton Public Library and the information services officer of the Halifax City Regional Library for their assistance in locating many of the biographies and magazine articles used in the preparation of this book. I have also to thank Demont Freeman of Amherst, N.S. for providing me with a copy of the Pauline Johnson Retrospective and Nicholas Tuele, curator of historical art at the Art Gallery of Greater Victoria, for so generously allowing me to include reproductions of Emily Carr's "Big Eagle, Skidigate, B.C." and "Sea and Sky." I am also indebted to Louise Guay-Bourassa of the Public Archives of Canada for her diligence in tracing photographs of Judy LaMarsh, Maude Abbott, L.M. Montgomery, Pauline Johnson, Mary Pickford, Karen Kain, Barbara Ann Scott, Mazo de la Roche and Emily Carr, and to K.R. Macpherson of the Archives of Ontario for locating the rare photograph of Laura Secord. I am also grateful to J. Thomas West of Canada's Sports Hall of Fame for permission to reproduce the photograph of Barbara Ann Scott and to Pamela Verrill Walker for permission to include the photograph of Judy LaMarsh.

But above all, my thanks go to my husband for the faith, support, patience and understanding that have helped make the doubts I have experienced disappear.

FOREWORD

The ten women included in this book represent — to me — a cross section of the most interesting women in Canadian history. From the moment I conceived the idea of writing a series of biographical profiles, their names came spontaneously to me. There was no question of making additions, deletions or substitutions. Another writer might have chosen ten entirely different women, but for me these were the ten who best exemplified the courage, singleness of purpose and enduring faith that make legendary a living, breathing human being.

November, 1983   Carol McLeod

CONTENTS

EMILY CARR

She sat alone beside the kennel, staring lovingly at the dog inside. His eyes pleaded with her to open the door and run with him through the pasture and into the fields beyond. But Emily was not in the mood for play. With a gleam in her eye, she scrambled to her feet and hurried back to the house.

Alone in her room, she rifled through her bureau searching madly for pencil and paper. Nothing! She slammed the drawers and tapped her foot in vexation. There had to be something! Suddenly, she spied the brown paper bag on the edge of the mantle. A box of candy from her father still nestled inside. She climbed on a chair and took down the bag. It was wrinkled and rough, but it would do. She took out the box, then sat down on the floor and reached in the grate. A charred piece of kindling would serve as a pencil. With a few deft strokes she sketched out a dog.

When she was finished, she propped up the paper on the back of a chair and peered at it closely. To her childish eyes it looked exactly like Carlow. She wondered what her father would think. With a pounding heart, she picked up the bag and flew down the stairs.

Her married sister, who was talking in the drawing room with her mother and father, looked down at the picture Emily had spread out so carefully over father's newspaper. "Why, that's not half bad!"

Richard Carr furrowed his brow. Before he could say anything his wife glanced down at Emily's hands. "Why, Emily you're filthy!" She pointed towards the kitchen. "I think we'd better go and get you cleaned up."

When the two had gone, Richard Carr folded the drawing and wrote on the back: "By Emily, age eight." He put it away among his personal papers and it was not seen again until after he died many years later. What there was about the sketch he felt was worth saving is impossible to say. It was crude and raw, but in his mind it was a start and a little while later Emily began to take drawing lessons.

Richard Carr had made a sizeable fortune during the early days of the California gold rush. In 1855 he returned to his native England and married Emily Saunders, a young English woman he had met in San Francisco. The couple returned to California and lived there for several years before deciding in 1861 to go back to England and settle in Devonshire. They bought a house in Barnstaple and tried to adapt to the leisured life style. But Richard's wandering spirit demanded more, and in 1863 he decided to emigrate to British Columbia. When they arrived in Victoria he opened a wholesale warehouse in the commercial section along Wharf Street and built an elegant Italianate villa for his growing family in a fashionable neighbourhood near Beacon Hill Park.

Three sons born to Richard and Emily Carr had died in infancy. The rest of the family was divided into two distinct parts: the older family, which consisted of two daughters; and the younger family, which consisted of three girls and a boy. Emily, who was born on December 13, 1871, was the eighth of the nine children.

Her childhood was a mixture of love and rejection. Richard Carr, autocratic and stern, ruled both at work and at home with an iron fist. Each child was a matter of total indifference to him until it became old enough to walk. From that time on, he or she was given a turn at being Richard's especial favourite. As soon as signs of self will set in, however, the child was dismissed and the next was chosen to take his place.

Emily, the youngest girl, was her father's last and most enduring favourite. Her younger brother, delicate from birth, was of no interest to Richard Carr and Emily's reign ran uninterrupted for many years. She was at her father's side whenever he was home and enjoyed her special closeness with him until the day in early puberty when a mysterious rift, never fully explained by Emily in later life, developed between them. After that, Emily resented her father's sternness.

She had just begun to devise methods of avoiding any

contact with him when her mother, who had been ill ever since the birth of her last child, died of tuberculosis. Emily was only 14 at the time, but she was mature enough to realize how deeply the loss affected her father. He retired from the business and died two years later, in 1888.

Suddenly Emily's life was turned upside down. Her eldest sister, Edith, almost twenty years older than the youngest child, took charge of the family. Her rule was hard and tyrannical, untempered by the justice that had made her father's rule endurable. Emily rebelled against the bitter discipline and spent the next two years at war with Edith. She fought not only her own battles, but also those of her brothers and sisters and was brutally whipped for her efforts. Her only solace came from the rides she took into the forest on the family's pony. Alone in the solitude of nature, she discovered the foundation on which she would build her life as a painter.

To those outside the family, the Carrs seemed to be a model of perfect harmony. Indeed, with the exception of Emily who was stubborn and unruly, the others managed to get along. Emily was the apple of discord: no one could understand her and no one could appreciate her spirit.

By the time she was 18, Emily realized she could no longer live at home. She went to James Lawson, the man her father had appointed guardian, and asked permission to study at the California School of Design in San Francisco. (Later known as the Mark Hopkins Institute of Art). To her surprise, Lawson consented and late in the summer of 1891 she sailed from California. She threw herself into her studies and for the next two and a half years her life revolved around her painting. Her still life professor took a special interest in her. He recognized her potential and discovered early in his association with her that her best only came to the fore when she was made angry enough to push it out.

During her years in San Francisco, Emily made friends with many of the students at the school and for the first time in her life, free from the tyranny of her father and sister, she was able to relax. Her new found peace affected her work and she gradually discovered she was making progress. The outdoor sketching classes became her favourite and she found a certain abstract quality in landscapes that was more compatible with her nature than the concrete exactness of still life. Her work was not spectacular, but it *did* show promise. Then, in the fall of 1893 she received a letter from Lawson telling her to come home.

She returned to Victoria in time for Christmas and for the first few weeks life was bearable. Her future, however, was uncertain and after the New Year she began to grow restless. Finally, a group of mothers heard that Emily was back. There were no art teachers at that time in the entire city and the group approached Emily and asked if she would give lessons to their children. At first Emily hesitated. The idea of standing up before her own pupils terrified her, but she missed the rhythm of life at school and in the end she agreed.

Her first classes were held in the Carr family dining room and for a few weeks things ran smoothly. But the lighting was poor and the mess left behind after the lessons were over did little to improve Edith's humour. Emily decided to move to the barn. It was brighter and roomier and out of the way. She asked Edith for permission to repair the loft and received an emphatic no. However, when Edith realized Emily was prepared to pay for the renovations, she grudgingly agreed.

For the next few years Emily continued with her teaching. Her pupils were, for the most part, responsive and bright, and instructing them managed to satisfy her. Gradually the restlessness she had experienced when she came home from San Francisco returned. She needed more formal training and her only hope was to study abroad.

She had just begun in 1898 to make plans for a trip to the Continent when a missionary friend of her sister, Lizzie, suggested that Emily go to the Ucluelet Mission on the west coast of Vancouver Island to experience the Indians and the isolation. It seemed like a good opportunity to sketch, so Emily packed up her gear and delayed her trip abroad.

Without realizing it, she had made a decision that would mould the future course of her life. The stark, almost meager life at the Ucluelet Mission both haunted and restored her. The vastness and loneliness of the landscape awakened a longing deep within her, and forever after landscapes were the main focus of her work. But during her entire stay at Ucluelet, she painted nothing. She knew she was not yet skilled enough to capture the enormity of what she saw.

When she returned to Victoria she applied for admission to the Westminster School of Art in London. While she waited for her reply, she discovered two things for the very first time: love and poetry. Of the two, she preferred poetry: it offered more and demanded less. She could take a book of poems with her to the woods and walk home refreshed. Love was a different matter. She gave it where it was not wanted, then had it given to her when she did not want it.

It came as a double relief when the letter finally arrived from London accepting her as a student. She made a few hurried preparations and left for England in the summer of 1899.

Once settled, she put all thoughts of romance behind her. She was there to learn and that was what she would do. But it was not easy. The crowds and confusion of London were anathema to her and she longed for the vastness of her western forests.

She was fighting stubbornly against her homesickness when she encountered a distraction that barred all thought of British Columbia from her mind for several weeks. A foot injury she had suffered years before began to cause her severe pain and by the time she had it seen to she had both a dislocated toe and a split bone. The doctor recommended amputation and Emily, anxious to get back to her classes, decided to follow his advice. The operation went smoothly, but in the days that followed she suffered worse pain than she had before. It was months before she could touch her foot without regretting the loss of her toe.

She had no sooner recovered than she found herself face to face with a second, more nagging distraction. William Paddon, the man she had rejected in Canada, had travelled to London to make another offer of marriage. Emily was furious. She thought she had made her feelings clear. However, when she saw him for the first time on the platform of Euston Station, it was as though he had brought a breath of British Columbia with him. For the next three months she and Paddon explored London and at times she actually enjoyed herself. But the constant stream of marriage proposals began to pall on her and finally, in a fit of desperation, she asked Paddon to go home. He winced, but agreed. He could not accept the fact that her work was the most important thing in her life, but he could, after three months, accept the fact that his proposals were bouncing off a brick wall.

Emily threw herself back into her painting. Often she was discouraged. Not once during her entire stay did one member of her family ask about her work in their letters. For her part, Emily was beginning to think she had made a mistake in choosing London as a place to study. The art trend at Westminster was largely conservative and seemed at odds with her natural style. She began to look for another school.

In the end she went to Cornwall and studied for eight months at the Julius Olsson Studio. Her relationship with Olsson was marked by a mutual antagonism, but Emily respected him for his talent and for the industry he demanded from his students.

In 1902 she studied with John Whiteley at The Meadows Studio in Hertfordshire. She was being drawn more and more towards landscape painting and in a little wood behind the main studio she worked on her form.

As the autumn of 1902 drew on she returned to London to collect winter clothing from a trunk she had stored in her former boarding house. On her first night back she collapsed. Friends she had made during her time at Westminster rallied around her and for the next six weeks she was confined to bed with an illness variously described as bronchitis, influenza, homesickness, fatigue and a reaction to city living.

She had just started to recover when she suffered a severe relapse. The long years of tension and study had taken their toll and she was sent to a sanitarium where she remained, unable to work, for the next eighteen months. When she had fully recuperated, she was allowed to go back to The Meadows Studio. But her energy lagged and her work was not up to its usual standard. Finally, after five and a half years, she decided she had had enough. She was going home.

Before she got to Victoria, she stopped in Cariboo, B.C. to visit friends — a man and woman who had been married while she was in England. The richness of the countryside restored Emily and she roamed the land, breathing in the soul and strength of the western forests.

When winter came, she moved on to Victoria. Nothing

14

had changed. Her sisters were still as foreign to her as they always had been. To escape the tension that soon built up, she fled to the woods and spent entire afternoons alone, thinking in the wilderness. After a few weeks she began to give art lessons and was hired as a cartoonist for "The Week," but they were only stopgap measures and she knew she would have to establish roots.

She was still considering the paths open to her when a delegation from the Ladies' Art Club of Vancouver contacted her late in 1905 and asked if she would be interested in teaching some of its members the basics of painting. It meant moving to Vancouver and living away from her sisters so Emily agreed. It was a mistake. She expected her students, wealthy women from society's elite, to tackle their studies with the same verve she had in London. When she discovered they were there to do what they wanted and not what she directed, she balked. On February 28, 1906, at the end of the first month, she was fired.

Emily took it in stride. The dilettantism of the Ladies' Art Club had disgusted her and she was glad to be free. She rented a studio on Granville Street and vowed to remain in Vancouver.

Actually, the ladies had done her a favour. Their smugness and arrogance had starched her energy and she attacked her work with renewed vigour. To her amazement, she discovered that her years in England had paid off after all. She *had* learned something. Her style was still too narrow, too conservative to capture the vastness of the western forest, but still, it had grown.

She surrounded herself with a menagerie of birds and animals and settled into a new routine. Before long she opened an art school and the enrollment encouraged her. Ignoring the method in Vancouver of teaching from flat copy, she took her pupils on long field trips and insisted they paint from life.

In her free time she took her sketch book and went with her dog into the forests and Indian villages of Vancouver Island. Her work continued to improve, but it was still not right. Then, on a pleasure trip to Alaska in 1907, she met T.J. Richardson, an American artist who was deeply moved by a sketch he saw her doing. He told her that she had captured the Indian flavour he had been searching for for years. His

15

encouragement spurred Emily and she soon made an important decision: she would paint a complete collection of totem poles in village settings. On several successive summers she journeyed to out-of-the-way places to sketch the material she needed. Her style began to loosen. The formality and conservatism she had learned in England began to disappear as she lost herself in the more direct and spiritual world of Indian art.

During the winters she continued with her teaching and actually found herself making money. In 1910 she decided to take some of her savings and go to France to study the new techniques in painting. A friend gave her a letter of introduction to an artist of the new school, Harry Gibb, and when Emily arrived in Paris she contacted him immediately. His paintings were vivid and intense and the cleanness and boldness of his landscapes intrigued her. He suggested that she study at the Académie Colarossi.

Emily followed his advice and went about her studies with the same industry she had in England. This time she saw immediate results. Colarossi encouraged her and discovered that she had a natural sense of colour. After about a month, however, she left Colarossi and went to study with a Scottish artist, John D. Fergusson.

A few weeks later she became ill. The oppressive confinement of the studios, combined with the noise and turmoil of the city had taken its toll and she was in hospital three months. It was late fall by the time she was released and she decided to go to Sweden for the winter.

When she returned to France in the spring, she joined a landscape class that Gibb had opened outside Paris. Once she had settled in, she showed Gibb some of her Indian sketches and he began to take an interest. He praised her colour sense and was impressed by her method of applying paint to canvas. He believed the things she could learn from him would help her express the vastness of the west and he helped her discover the way in which the pure colour, simplified form and distorted perspective of the fauvist movement could convey emotion. His criticism of the work she did was terse and to the point, but he believed she had the talent to make a name for herself.

She painted in the open fields incorporating fauvist

elements in her style from early morning until it was too dark to see. Gibb warned her she was working too hard but she refused to listen. For months she kept up a gruelling pace. Then, one day she discovered she had gone dry. She needed something new.

Frances Hodgkins, a water colourist from New Zealand, was teaching at Concarneau and Emily decided to go and study with her for six weeks. The change of medium and environment did her good and at the end of the six weeks she felt completely refreshed — ready to return to British Columbia. Her year and a half in France had strengthened her style and broadened her insight, but she still had doubts about her ability to capture the spirit of the western forests.

When she returned to Canada in December, 1911 she visited with her sisters in Victoria, then continued on to Vancouver and opened a new studio. In the spring of 1912 she held an exhibition of the work she had done in France. Over all, the reception of her unique style, foreign as it was to the conservative tastes of the people of Vancouver, was favourable. Yet Emily seized upon the negative comments and seemed to ignore the positive. The rejection she perceived stung her deeply, but she continued — for a little longer — to believe in what she was doing.

Later that year the British Columbia Society of Fine Arts invited her to show her work at their annual exhibition. Of the ten paintings she submitted to the hanging committee, two were rejected and Emily withdrew the entire collection. She entered a state of extreme depression and saw only a slight lifting of spirits when she took out some of her old sketches and compared them with her new ones. Her work had grown, but she had not grown with it.

In the fall she moved back to Victoria. It was the same old story. Her sisters could not understand her and this time they considered Emily and her art a family disgrace. For Emily it was the final blow. She could not live on the proceeds of her art and she *would* not live in the same house with her sisters. There had to be another route.

Taking a lot of land she had inherited from her father, she borrowed money and built a four suite apartment building. She equipped one suite with a studio and rented out the others.

17

The income, she hoped, would be enough to get by on. But Emily had not forseen the outbreak of World War I. Rentals sank and taxes rose. There was no longer enough money for her to cover her expenses.

Finally, she turned to pottery making. Tourists gobbled up the little pieces decorated with Indian designs and Emily turned them out by the hundreds. She loathed herself for prostituting Indian art, but she had no choice. Her reduced circumstances and the rejection she had felt as the result of the exhibitions had destroyed her self-confidence and she vowed never to paint again.

She was in a downward spiral and she had not yet touched bottom. Her rental income shrank even further as the war continued and in 1916 she redid the top floor of her apartment building and turned it into a boarding house for women.

The resulting lack of privacy and the constant demands of a gaggle of bad-tempered old maids rankled Emily more than anything had ever rankled her before. Her only solace came in 1917 when she combined her love of animals with her need for money and established a kennel of Bobtail Sheep Dogs on land behind her garden. The work was a source of pure pleasure for her and over the years she raised more than 350 puppies.

Following the war, her life remained a tangle of housekeeping, pottery making and wrangles with her sisters. In 1924 she began to exhibit her work again, but it was not until 1927 that she regained any momentum in her life. In the summer of that year she received a telephone call from a man she had never heard of. He was Eric Brown of the National Gallery of Canada; he had heard about her work and wanted to include it in an exhibition of West Coast Indian Art the gallery was holding in Ottawa. It was the opportunity of a lifetime and Emily agreed. She felt it marked a new stage in her development and to record the changes she foresaw in her life she started a journal, which she maintained on a sporadic basis for the next fourteen years.

In November, 1927, on her way east to attend the showing, she stopped off in Toronto. She had heard of the Group of Seven — seven men who were revolutionizing

Canadian art — and she was eager to meet them. Their work was bold and innovative and it appealed to Emily as no art ever had. She established a friendship with Lawren Harris, one of the group's leading members, and with his encouragement decided that her fifteen years away from the easel had come to an end.

Three days after she returned to Victoria she was back at her work and that summer she went to the Indian villages to sketch. But time had not been kind. Fifteen years had brought decay to the old Indian way of life and the villages were no longer a source of inspiration to her. She concentrated instead on the verdant stillness of the forest. Her trips renewed and revitalized her and she began to take along a notebook so she could etch in words the feelings she wanted to convey in oil.

Two of her canvasses were included by the Group of Seven in an eastern exhibition and her work was soon after shown to favourable reviews in Toronto, Ottawa, Montreal and Washington. Her output increased and she began to capture not only the power and vitality of the forests, but also their agelessness and vulnerability. Her style, with its unusual mixture of aloofness and subjectivity, was a wholly unique fusion of fauvism, cubism and impressionism that was rich in its understanding and alive in its dynamism. Lawren Harris wrote: "The pictures are works of art in their own right . . . (they) have creative life in them . . . they breathe." .

Emily was alive as she had never been before. Her reputation grew and spread and her paintings began to sell all across the country. Then, early in 1937 she suffered a major setback. A pain she had experienced intermittently for several years finally attacked with vengeance. It was her heart, and she was ordered to bed. The menagerie that she had collected over the years was reluctantly disbanded and her easel was put away.

For weeks Emily languished in a hospital bed, unable to do anything. Painting was forbidden — at least for the present — and she longed to be busy. At last she remembered her writing. In 1934 she had taken a course in short story writing, and now, with nothing to do, the notebooks she had filled in the woods suddenly took on new meaning. With her doctor's consent, she began to write of those things in life which had touched her most deeply. She gathered together a collection of

19

stories from her days with the Indians and called it *Klee Wyck (Laughing One)*. The work soothed her and she soon started an autobiography.

When she returned home from the hospital she sent the book off to a publisher. For months she heard nothing; then she was told the manuscript had been lost. She was furious — she had sent them her only copy and she was determined to get it back. One letter to the publisher followed another until at last the manuscript was found and returned.

Ira Dilworth, who later became Professor of English at the University of British Columbia, eventually heard about the stories and suggested that a series of six be read on the radio. Emily agreed and the first series, read by Dr. G.G. Sedgewick of the University of British Columbia, was followed by a second read by Ira Dilworth and the stories soon attracted the attention of an eastern publisher.

Klee Wyck was published a few days before Emily's 70th birthday. The reviews were excellent and the book was awarded the 1941 Governor General's medal for nonfiction. A year later *The Book of Small* appeared. The first section was devoted to anecdotes from Emily's own childhood while the second section dealt with the early days of Victoria. Reviews were as favourable as they had been for *Klee Wyck* and *The Book of Small* was followed by several more books. *The House of All Sorts,* a collection of stories about her dogs and her experiences as a landlady, appeared in 1944. *Growing Pains,* her autobiography, was published posthumously in 1946 and was followed by *Pause: A Sketch Book* and *The Heart of a Peacock* both in 1953. *Hundreds and Thousands,* which contained excerpts from her private journals, was published in 1966.

The success of her writing pleased Emily, but writing was not her first love and she was anxious to get back to her easel. In spite of her doctor's warnings not to overtire herself, she journeyed to the woods with her sketch book several more times between 1938 and 1940. She rented a cabin and took along a maid, but it was still too much for her. The paintings, although good, were not up to the standard she had set in the past. On her last foray the strain was too much and she suffered a relapse. Her heart condition was aggravated by liver and gall bladder trouble and she suffered greatly from rheumatism. Her health continued to deteriorate and during her last illness she had her personal keepsakes sorted and buried, Indian fashion, in the forest. Early in 1945 she was notified that the University of British Columbia intended to confer an honorary Doctor of Letters degree upon her at the May convocation. She was filled with a deep sense of pride, but the honour came too late. She died on March 2, 1945.

E. PAULINE JOHNSON

The sun had just dipped below the horizon when the surrey carrying George and Emily Johnson home from Brantford turned into the tree-lined drive. Pauline, who had been watching for her parents from an upstairs window, smiled happily, then leaned forward, rested her brow against the cool glass and closed her eyes.

In her mind she pictured the way the gently rolling lawns and the well-wooded park must have looked on that August night many years before when her mother and father had come home to "Chiefswood" for the first time.

Her mother had told her how beautiful the house had looked, bathed in the glow of the blazing sunset, and how excited she had been that the stuccoed colonial mansion was to be her new home. Pauline's eyes crinkled with pleasure as she pictured her strong, athletic father lifting his tiny bride down from the surrey. He must have been very proud.

Then, suddenly, a frown clouded Pauline's face. It always did when she remembered the story her mother had told about the bickering that had gone on before her wedding. Most of her relatives had been appalled that Emily would even consider marrying an Indian, and George's parents had been even more appalled when they discovered that their oldest son was going to marry a white woman. But George and Emily had ignored the squabbling; they loved each other, and that was enough.

Pauline sighed and looked again out the window. The surrey had just pulled up. There was a clatter in the hallway as her sister and two brothers rushed down the stairs to greet their parents. Pauline smoothed back her long black hair, then turned and hurried off to join them.

On her father's side, Pauline Johnson was a member of

the Mohawk aristocracy. She was a direct descendant of one of the five chiefs who had banded their Mohawk, Oneida, Onandaga, Seneca and Cayuga tribes together during the 16th century to form the Brotherhood of the Five Nations. A sixth tribe, the Tuscarora, had later joined, changing the name of the confederation to the Brotherhood of the Six Nations.

Her original family name, Tekahionwake, (which means "double wampum") fell into disuse after her great-grandfather was baptized in the late 1700s and adopted the name Johnson from the man who acted as his godfather, Sir William Johnson.

Pauline's grandfather, Smoke Johnson, served with great distinction fighting for the British during the War of 1812. He was noted for his powerful oratory and was often referred to as "The Mohawk Warbler." He married a descendant of one of the great chiefs who had composed the first federal council of the Five Nations and their eldest son, George (Pauline's father), eventually inherited the title of chief.

As a boy, George Johnson attended the Mohawk Institute School for Children on the outskirts of Brantford. He made great progress with his studies and showed such a marked proficiency in languages that when Adam Elliott, the new Anglican missionary arrived on the Six Nations Reservation in 1837, he asked George to serve as his assistant and interpreter. George accepted the offer and soon after became a member of the Elliott household. During his years with the Elliotts, he learned much of English manners and etiquette and acquired the poise and grace of a true gentleman. He spoke and read English, French, German, Mohawk and the five other languages of the Six Nations, and in 1840 he was appointed official interpreter for the English Church Mission on the reserve. In 1853 he married Emily Howells, a well-bred English woman who had moved to the mission after her sister married Adam Elliott.

To provide a suitable home for his new wife, Johnson bought a 200 acre estate on the reservation, and from the proceeds of a profitable investment he had made several years earlier, built a lavish home and furnished it in the English fashion.

The snubs he and Emily received from their families

because of their mixed marriage did not affect the pleasure they found in their life together and it was not until the birth of their first child that they came face to face with their first real obstacle. The title of "chief" had been passed down from one generation of George's mother's family to the next, but because Emily was white, her first son, Henry Beverly, could not inherit it. The refusal of the tribe to accept Beverly (he was called by his second name) as their future chief was made even more bitter for George and Emily by the fact that by law Beverly was considered an Indian. Ironically, the tribe would later acknowledge George and Emily's daughters as Mohawk princesses.

The blow of seeing their son deprived of his birthright was softened, however, a few weeks after his birth when Emily's father arrived unexpectedly to see his new grandson. Once Mr. Howells met Beverly and his son-in-law and took in the grandeur of "Chiefswood," all hostility disappeared. About a year later, the Johnsons dropped their animosity towards their daughter-in-law and George and Emily's happiness was complete. Two more children, a daughter Evelyn and a son Allen, followed Beverly in quick succession, and on March 10, 1861 Emily gave birth to her last child, a daughter, Emily Pauline.

As the youngest of the family, Pauline received a never ending shower of attention. She was brought up on the poems of Keats and Byron, and by the time she was 12 she had read the complete works of Scott and Longfellow and had made great inroads with Shakespeare and Emerson.

But her influences were not entirely English. Like her brothers and sister she was brought up to respect her Indian heritage and the Mohawk culture became an important part of her life.

During her early years, Pauline received her education at home from her mother and her grandfather, Smoke Johnson. Her mother focused on literature and the domestic arts, while her grandfather concentrated on the history and legends of the Mohawk people. When she was 10, the finer parts of her education were undertaken by a governess and when she was 12 Pauline, who had become a voracious reader, began three years of study at the Indian day school on the reservation.

She had many interests in common with her father and she was very proud of him. His speaking ability and his relentless efforts against the erosion of the Mohawk culture by white whiskey traders had brought him to the attention of the federal government. Dressed in full Mohawk regalia, he had addressed the Senate, House of Commons, and the Governor General on several occasions to fight for justice and his people.

On the long walks he and Pauline used to take together through the forests of the reservation, he instilled in her an interest and respect for nature. But for Pauline the time they spent together was much too short. He was often busy looking after the affairs of his people and when he was free to be with her, he was often ill. A savage beating he had received when Pauline was four had left him with a crushed skull, a broken upper jaw, a splintered lower jaw and a badly injured back. White men had attacked him as he tried to intercept a load of whiskey that was being hauled to the reservation and had left him for dead. One of the men involved in the beating was later sentenced to seven years in Kingston Penitentiary, and although Johnson partially recovered, he suffered after effects for the rest of his life.

Politically, however, the attack had left him undeterred and he continued to fight for his people. Social honours were heaped upon him in recognition of his efforts and "Chiefswood," his elegant estate, began to receive a series of distinguished visitors. Royalty, military leaders, politicians, scholars, writers and artists all paid visits to the Johnsons at one time or another and all left knowing that Johnson, who was every inch an Indian, was also every inch a gentleman.

Pauline's exposure to her parents' distinguished guests helped her develop poise and charm and by the time she was 16 she had the sophistication and general knowledge of many adults. But the Johnsons realized that Pauline's life could not revolve totally around "Chiefswood." In the fall of 1877, they decided the time had come to send her away to school. They did not want to send her far, but they *did* want her to experience life outside the reservation. Central Collegiate in Brantford seemed the perfect answer. It was 18 miles from "Chiefswood" and far enough away that Pauline would have to live in the city. Friends of the Johnsons in Brantford offered to let her stay with them and for the next two years Pauline attended public school.

As an Indian in a white community she was defensive for a time of her Mohawk heritage. Gradually, however, she grew accustomed to her new surroundings and with her ready wit and skillful repartee she soon won a wide range of friends.

In her spare time she continued to read a great deal and occasionally she took a canoe and paddled alone on Grand River. It was during this period of her life that Pauline began to experience moments of deep introspection and she started to write brief passages of poetry. On vacations at "Chiefswood" she was able to share her feelings with her brother, Allen, who was closest to her in age. They shared a love of nature and some of their happiest moments together were spent canoeing on Grand River.

In 1897 Pauline left Central Collegiate and returned home to "Chiefswood." For the next five years she enjoyed a life of ease and she spent much of her time reading, writing poetry and canoeing. Then, in 1884 her father died and life took a drastic change. Mrs. Johnson soon discovered that she could no longer afford the upkeep of "Chiefswood" and she moved into lodgings in Brantford. Allen and Beverly were both on their own, one working in Hamilton and the other in Toronto, but Evelyn and Pauline went with their mother. Evelyn found a job with the Indian Office and Pauline realized that she too would have to find some way to contribute to her mother's support.

Friends suggested that she submit her poems to magazines. At first Pauline hesitated. Many of them were personal reflections written for her own pleasure. In the end, however, she sent some off and in 1885 "My Little Jean" was published by the American magazine *Gems of Poetry*. Later that same year a Canadian magazine, *The Week* (which was at that time edited by Charles G.D. Roberts), bought another of her poems and Pauline soon had her work accepted by many other magazines.

In 1886 the city of Brantford unveiled a statue to its eponym, the famous Mohawk chief, Joseph Brant, and Pauline was asked to compose a suitable poem and recite it at

26

the dedication ceremonies. The writing of the poem presented no difficulty, but reading it was another matter entirely. At the final moment she was too nervous to deliver it and a local dignitary was hurriedly chosen to do it for her.

For the next several years Pauline continued to write. A number of magazines began to buy her work on a regular basis and in 1889 two of her poems appeared in the prestigious Canadian anthology *Songs of the Great Dominion*. The well-known English critic, Theodore Watts-Dunton was impressed by the poems Pauline had contributed to the anthology and declared Pauline a poet "full of the spirit of the open air." In 1891 John Greenleaf Whittier wrote to Pauline praising her poems for their strength and beauty and pointing out the opportunities that lay ahead.

Yet, despite her success in finding publishers for her work, Pauline found it impossible to support herself, let alone contribute to the support of her mother. Rates paid for poetry were ridiculously low (her manager was later to say that she made less than $500 from her poetry during her lifetime) and as a woman of 30, Pauline realized she had to find another way.

Finally, in January, 1892 a door opened. The Young Liberal Club of Toronto was holding an "All Authors Night" and Pauline was invited to read her poetry. The evening got off to a poor start and by the time Pauline appeared on the stage, the audience had begun to fidget. As she stood alone beneath the glaring spotlight she experienced a moment of sheer panic. Then, suddenly, a burst of confidence welled through her and she recited her poetry with a verve and passion that stirred her audience and won it over. Frank Yeigh, the organizer of the event, quickly recognized Pauline's potential and asked if she would be interested in performing again. She agreed and on February 19 she appeared to an even greater ovation at Association Hall. A review which appeared in the *Toronto Globe* on February 20 said her recitation had "a touch of pathos that gave the reader a chance to exercise her musical and flexible voice most effectively." More performances were scheduled and Pauline was on her way.

Certainly the time was right. Few cities in Canada enjoyed live theater and the day of motion pictures had yet to dawn. The only source of entertainment was touring artists who went from town to town performing in whatever out-of-the-way hall was available. The tours were often highly profitable and over the next few months Pauline made 125 appearances throughout Ontario and Quebec.

Her natural charm and dignity combined with her innate dramatic ability and poetic talent, turned her readings into events that people long remembered. Her grace and poise warmed the audiences and her depth of feeling and unaffected manner enabled her to deliver both fire and softness with equal ease. The solitude she had experienced during her years on the reservation, however, had never really prepared her for the outside world and each performance became a test of acceptance. More than the money and critical acclaim, she wanted to be accepted as a person and her audiences accepted her completely.

Mrs. Johnson was deeply moved by Pauline's poetry and was proud of Pauline's success both as a poet and a performer. When the inevitable criticism came from friends and relatives that performing on a stage was undignified, Pauline and her mother bridled in unison. Spurred by her mother's example of defying convention to marry a man of a different race, Pauline carried on and in time most of her relatives came to accept her new profession. The one holdout — Pauline's sister Evelyn — denounced Pauline as an undesirable and refused to have anything more to do with her.

Success followed success and by 1894 Pauline had earned enough money to go to England. Her first book, *The White Wampum* was published in London during her stay and quickly became a critical success. Her love poems, intensely passionate and personal, were filled with an emotional spirit born of the fire of her soul, while her poems of nature (which were written from an Indian point of view) had a simple lyric quality that elevated them above the passion of the human spirit and somehow merged them with the eternal.

Her rhythmic style was a perfect match for the subject matter of her poems, while her rich but restrained imagery infused her work with a vibrant visual quality that enabled the reader to see as well as feel the spirit of each poem.

Her work was unique and she became an overnight sensation. Several prominent members of British society, who had met George Johnson during visits to Canada, took an interest in Pauline and hostesses began including her on their guest lists.

By the time Pauline started to give her performances, interest in her Indian heritage had reached unprecedented proportions and she decided to make the most of it. Using her Mohawk family name, Tekahionwake, and appearing in full Mohawk dress, she presented an image unlike anything the British had ever seen. Her readings were hugely popular and left the public clamouring for more.

By this time, Pauline had begun to write short stories and the well known British actor-manager, Sir George Alexander, approached her with the offer of turning her story "A Red Girl's Reasoning" into a full length drama. As it turned out, the story was too brief to be turned into a play, but it made an excellent dramatic sketch which Pauline later used in her tours of Canada.

Pauline returned to Brantford late in 1894. Her feelings about her trip were mixed. Although her book and performances had been well received, the book had made very little in the way of profit. Poetry just didn't seem to pay. She made more money from her prose and she soon began selling stories, sketches and articles to a wide variety of magazines. The proceeds from her writing and performances were now enough to support herself, but in order to contribute to her mother's support she could not relax her pace.

Immediately after she returned from England she began a tour of Canada that took her from one end of the country to the other. Her belief in a united Canada, combined with her dramatic fervour, roused audiences to displays of patriotism unseen for many years, and her name soon became a household word.

In 1897 she met Walter McRaye, a professional entertainer, and appeared with him, reciting poetry in a number of Canadian cities. When Pauline returned to Brantford in January, 1898 she astounded her family by announcing her engagement to Charles Drayton, an assistant inspector with the Western Loan and Savings Company of Winnipeg.

A few months later her mother died and Pauline was

badly shaken. Up until that time she had considered Brantford her home. But now, without her mother, she could see no point in staying. Allen, her favourite brother, was working for the Canada Life Assurance Company in Toronto and Beverly was working for the North American Life Insurance Company in Montreal. Evelyn was still in Brantford, but that meant nothing to Pauline. The only tie she had left to Brantford was "Chiefswood" and although the house was still empty, Pauline could not afford to reopen it.

Finally, in July she announced that she and Drayton would be married in Winnipeg and would take up residence there. But she did not anounce a date for the wedding. Then, suddenly, and without a word of explanation, she announced that the engagement had been broken. She refused for ever after to discuss the matter and for a time she withdrew into herself. But as the year dragged on, she began to make plans for another cross country tour and early in 1898, accompanied once again by Walter McRaye, she went to Ottawa for her opening performance. McRaye soon became her personal manager and as they crossed and recrossed the country during the next few years, he also became a close friend and confidant.

Her schedule was hectic, but in what spare time she had, Pauline continued with her writing. However, the pressures of her constant travelling eventually reduced the quality of her work and much of her later poetry dealt with contemporary issues that appealed to the audiences but not the critics.

In 1906 Pauline and McRaye went to England and opened their tour to good reviews at London's Steinway Hall. During their stay they met Chief Joe of the Capilano tribe of Squamish Indians, who was there from British Columbia on behalf of his people to present a grievance to the king.

In 1907 Pauline made a third and final trip to England following which, in 1909, she settled down in Vancouver for a long overdue rest. There she met again with Chief Joe and learned from him many of the legends of the west coast Indians. Using her unique literary style, she embellished the stories and preserved them for future generations. The stories, which were serialized by the Vancouver "Province," were a huge success and were perhaps her most enduring contribution to Canadian literature.

By 1910, however, her output began to decline. She was ill and in pain and the doctors diagnosed cancer of the breast. Her condition was inoperable and drugs had to be prescribed to control the pain.

Her many expenses soon began to eat away at her savings and, to help, a group of friends collected her west coast Indian stories and published them together in a book entitled *Legends of Vancouver*. The book sold well and after the first three limited editions had been published in Vancouver, McClelland and Stewart of Toronto bought the copyright in 1912 and produced a larger fourth edition. That same year *The White Wampum*, which had originally been published in 1894, and *Canadian Born*, which had been published in 1903, were combined by the Musson Book Company of Toronto and published under the title (chosen by Pauline) of *Flint and Feather*.

By May, 1912 Pauline's condition had deteriorated to the point that she was forced to enter a private hospital in Vancouver. Evelyn, realizing how ill Pauline really was, went to Vancouver because she felt it was her duty to represent the family at Pauline's deathbed. A few meetings between the two did not go well and Evelyn returned home.

Her doctors soon told Pauline that she had only a short time left. When the initial depression had passed, she returned to her poetry. *Fight On,* based on Tennyson's line "And he said fight on," is perhaps the most stirring and poignant of her many works. She tried diligently to complete a project she had long been contemplating — a series of ballads based on the folklore of the west coast Indians. She finished the first of the series late in 1912 and made a start on the second. But she was soon too ill to continue and she died on March 7, 1913 — three days before her 52nd birthday. Around her neck was a gold locket, which she had given instructions, was not to be opened or removed.

As she had requested, her body was cremated and her ashes, together with a copy of *Flint and Feather* and *Legends of Vancouver* were buried on a hill in Stanley Park overlooking the sea. On the Sunday following her death, a memorial service was held in the Mohawk chapel on the Six Nations Reservation near Brantford, and in the cemetery where her parents were buried, a cairn was erected in her memory.

MAUDE ABBOTT

With a sigh of contentment, Maude Abbott leaned back in the big, overstuffed armchair and picked up the book that had been lying on her lap. She hadn't looked at it for a long time and today she wanted to read some of the passages — just to remember what the longing had been like.

She flipped through the pages until she came to the section she was looking for: "March, 1884. One of my daydreams, which I feel to be selfish, is that of going to school . . .And here I go again; once (I) begin dreaming of the possibilities I become half daft over what I know will never come to pass. Oh, to *think* of studying with other girls! Think of learning German, Latin, and other languages in general. Think of the loveliness of thinking that it entirely depended on myself whether I got on... if I *were* to go to school, if it were for one term, how happy I would be."

"April 9. (If) I get my wish I will try to keep my resolutions (1) to study hard and conscientiously; (2) not to get wild, etc., as many girls do; (3) not to care for the competition, but for the real study and the benefit I will derive from it; (4) to remember that I go to school for education, not for fun."

"Dec. 28, 1884. I am just jotting a few lines to tell how my wish has come true, and I have gone to school, so now I have a chance to keep those resolutions I made a few pages back . . .We are never satisfied. My next wish is to go to college."

Maude Abbott was born in St. Andrews East, Quebec, on March 18, 1869. Her family name was actually Babin, but her father, the Reverend Jeremiah Babin, deserted his wife shortly before Maude was born and when Mrs. Babin died a few months later, Maude and her sister Alice were adopted by their maternal grandmother, Mrs. William Abbott. Mrs.

Abbott brought her two granddaughters up in a happy, upper middle class home and devoted herself to them.

The sting of losing her parents did not affect Maude during her childhood, but in later life she grew to regret the lack of a conventional upbringing. She saw her father from time to time, but their relationship was distant and she developed no affection for him whatsoever.

The greatest influence in her life was her grandmother, who, with her vibrant personality and gentle humour, helped mould Maude into a warmhearted, impulsive woman with a superabundance of spirit and determination.

The only other person to whom Maude was really close during her early years was her sister, Alice, and as time passed the two became inseparable. Maude was by far the stronger and even though she was the younger, she became a sort of surrogate mother to Alice.

The girls were educated at home during their childhood by a governess Mrs. Abbott had hired when they were very young. But as Maude grew older she longed to go away to school and in November 1884 Mrs. Abbott finally gave in and sent her to take her final year of high school at a private seminary in Montreal.

Maude made the most of her time and did so well that in June, 1885 she was awarded a scholarship to McGill University. The first class of women had been admitted to McGill only the year before and winning the scholarship was a truly great distinction.

Classes began in September and Maude tackled them with enthusiasm. She had only been in Montreal three weeks, however, when family matters forced her to return to St. Andrews. The following year she went back to McGill and in 1890 she graduated with the third class of women in arts.

When she had accepted the scholarship in 1885, the idea of studying medicine had not occurred to her. All she had wanted then was a well-rounded education. Her outlook changed, however, during her sophomore year when a friend commented that if she had not decided to become an artist, she would probably have been a doctor.

From that moment the idea of studying medicine took root in Maude's mind, and in February, 1889, while still in her

34

third year of arts, she wrote to the Faculty of Medicine at McGill (which at that time was independent of the University and steadfastly ignored the Faculty of Art's example of admitting women students) and requested that provision be made to enroll women in the near future.

Grace Ritchie (later Dr. Grace Ritchie England) had already been admitted to Queen's University in Kingston, where a course for the training of women in medicine had previously been established, but Maude was not interested in Queen's. Her heart was set on McGill, but as she had expected her request was flatly denied.

Maude immediately launched her attack and as friends rallied around her, the newspapers, sensing a story, took up the lead. They questioned a number of Montreal's leading physicians and found that although few actually opposed the concept of female doctors, many were concerned about the idea of mixed classes.

Dr. William Osler, a graduate of McGill, a former professor of pathology and physiology at the McGill School of Medicine, and a world renowned writer, teacher and clinician, wrote from the University of Pennsylvania saying that he could see no reason to oppose medical education for women, and that as far as mixed classes went, they had been taught in other universities without the world coming to an end.

But the Medical Faculty refused to budge and in the fall of 1890 Maude gave up the battle and enrolled in the medical school at the University of Bishop's College in Lennoxville near Montreal. It was the first year Bishop's had offered medical courses to women and Maude settled down to a gruelling regimen of classes and study.

In December her grandmother died and although Maude was badly shaken, she pulled herself back together and by January was back in her old routine. For the next few years she immersed herself in her work. But she longed to be back at McGill and in 1893 she wrote to the University requesting permission to attend lectures during the summer session. The answer was once again an emphatic "no".

McGill was totally intransigent and its attitude for a time threatened Maude's advancement at Bishop's. Montreal General Hospital was used by both Bishop's and McGill as a training ground to give medical students practical experience in the wards. Tickets of admission were granted as a matter of course to students attending the two universities. However, when Maude applied for hers, it was withheld. Grace Ritchie, who had transferred to Bishop's from Queen's, had been granted a ticket for the academic year 1890-91, but the committee issuing the tickets was influenced more by McGill than by Bishop's and it decided to deter future applications by women by making an example of Maude and denying her her ticket. The newspapers, getting wind of the story, once again rallied to Maude's side and after much public controversy, her ticket was finally issued.

Although the male students were for the most part respectful to Maude, she was very sensitive about her position as sole woman in the class and she was extremely lonely. Her shyness with strangers did nothing to endear her to her colleagues and the zeal and determination with which she went about her work was often resented by less inspired male students.

In June, 1894 she graduated with honours and was awarded the Senior Anatomy Prize and the Chancellor's Prize for final subjects. In July she left for Europe to do postgraduate study. Alice accompanied her and together they toured the continent for several weeks before settling in Zurich where Maude entered the university for the winter session and Alice studied music. A few months later they moved on to Vienna and stayed there for the next two years. Shortly after they arrived, Alice suffered a severe mental breakdown and despite Maude's insistence that she see the best doctors of the day, never fully recovered.

Despite the strain of Alice's illness, Maude drove herself on and enrolled in postgraduate courses in gynecology, obstetrics, and internal medicine. She soon developed a keen interest in internal medicine and pathology and began to see them as possible specialties.

In September, 1897 she returned to Canada and took Alice back to St. Andrews. Although Alice alternated between periods of lucidity and violence, Maude refused to put her in an institution. She hired a nurse to look after her and once she was certain the nurse would treat Alice kindly, she returned to

Montreal.

That November she opened her own office. But what she really wanted was to join the staff of the McGill Medical Faculty, and to advance her cause she wrote a paper on functional heart murmurs, which proved her powers in pathological research. However, the pleasure she had derived from the project quickly dissipated when she discovered that because women were not admitted to the Montreal Medico-Chirurgical Society, the paper would have to be read for her at the society's general meeting. She bore the indignity with grace and her tolerance was soon rewarded. Not only was the paper a huge success, but she was soon after elected as the first female member of the society.

Several other research papers drew equal attention and in recognition of her expertise in pathology she was appointed in the summer of 1898 to the position of curator of the medical musuem at McGill. Three years later she was promoted to the head curator's post and given the task of cataloguing the huge and growing collection of pathological specimens. Dr. William Osler, who was by then at John Hopkins University in Baltimore, heard of Maude's new responsibilities and when she travelled to nearby Washington to study the cataloguing system at the Army Medical Museum, met with her and fired her with the sense of the professional opportunities that lay ahead of her.

Over the next year she allowed her practice to drop off as she devoted herself more and more to pathology. She worked with unlimited fervour and as her responsibilities expanded, so did her interests and enthusiasm. Besides her cataloguing, she became involved in several projects sponsored by the Association of Medical Museums and also wrote articles on her pathological discoveries and observations. Yet, despite her hectic schedule, she still found time for a social life. The shyness of her earlier years had gradually disappeared and she loved to both entertain and be entertained. Her warm, self-effacing humour drew people to her and her sincerity and interest often made her the center of attention.

As her cataloguing progressed, she came across a specimen of a rare three-chambered heart. Its malformation intrigued her and she began to do extensive research on congenital heart disease. Osler heard of her research and in 1905 asked her to write the section on congenital heart disease for a book he was preparing. In spite of her already heavy workload, Maude agreed and within two years had written a lengthy article based on 421 autopsied cases, which Osler described as "the best thing ever written on the subject in English." Over the years she developed a close friendship with Osler and after he was knighted in 1911, she spent several weeks visiting with him and his wife in England.

When Osler died in December 1919, Maude decided to write a comprehensive article on his life for the International Association of Medical Museums. As had been the case with so many of her projects, the idea grew beyond its original concept and in the end she published a book of over six hundred pages.

In 1923 she was offered a one year term as Chief of Pathology at the Women's Medical College of Pennsylvania. Realizing the scope the position afforded, Maude obtained a leave of absence from McGill and completely reorganized the Department of Pathology at the College, greatly increasing its academic rating.

In recognition of her accomplishments, she was reappointed for a second term. She had many friends during her time at the college and her simple down to earth manner and warm humour endeared her to staff and students alike. Much to her delight, she was affectionately dubbed "The Big Chief of Hearts."

A colleague from her days in Pennsylvania recalled how on one particular occasion friends had gathered at a train station to see Maude off on a much awaited trip. Remembering something she had to show one of them, Maude unconcernedly opened her suitcase on the platform and had just begun to root for the special treasure when the train drew into the station and her friends had to frantically push her aside to repack the suitcase.

Maude returned to McGill in 1926 and took up her heavy workload and her writing with renewed zeal. Her articles dealt in great detail with the many unusual cases and specimens she had come across as a pathologist and many focused on congenital heart disease. When her *Atlas of*

Congenital Heart Disease was published by the American Heart Association in 1936 it was heralded as a valuable addition to medical knowledge.

Later in 1936 Maude celebrated her sixty-seventh birthday and, according to the laws and statues of McGill, she had no alternative but to retire. The thought of leaving the University and giving up her work was anathema to her and true to her warrior-like spirit she fought for an extension. But the Board of Regents at McGill was as unrelenting in 1936 about its retirement policy as it had been in 1889 about admitting women students to its Faculty of Medicine. However, the blow was softened somewhat when McGill announced that at the forthcoming convocation it was awarding Maude an honourary Doctor of Laws Degree, the highest honour the University had to bestow.

Two days after receiving the degree, Maude set off on an extensive seven week lecture tour of the Pacific Coast. The lectures were well attended and well received and during the next few months numerous honours were bestowed upon her, the most important of which to Maude was her election as an honourary member of the male only Osler Society at McGill University.

In 1937 she began work on a text book on congenital heart disease. She wrote to the Guggenheim Foundation applying for a fellowship and to John Hopkins Hospital in Baltimore asking permission to carry out research there if she received the fellowship. Permission was granted and although her fellowship was declined, she did receive a grant from the Carnegie Corporation, made on the recommendation of the secretary of the Guggenheim Foundation.

But the years were finally catching up with her and by early 1940 Maude had begun to experience unusual periods of drowziness and fatigue. Her enthusiasm for the text book uncharacteristically waned and in July she suffered a cerebral hemorrhage. She survived the initial crisis, but her condition continued to deteriorate and on September 2, 1940 she died at the age of 71.

LAURA SECORD

Laura stormed into the house and slammed her slate down on the kitchen table. With one angry tug she pulled out a chair and flung herself into it, then buried her head in her arms and began to sob.

"Why, Laura!" Mrs. Ingersoll exclaimed as she hurried into the kitchen. "Whatever's wrong?"

"Nothing." Laura peered up through a tangle of chestnut curls. "Just nothing."

"Well, I don't think that's quite true, now is it?"

Laura shrugged.

"Why don't you tell me about it," her mother said gently, "and maybe I can help."

Laura glanced up dubiously. Then, in a torrent, the words came tumbling out. "It's that Buster Morgan! Today Miss Charman told us about Joan of Arc and said she was a brave woman we should all remember and Buster and Willie said she was just a dumb girl who couldn't mind her own business."

Mrs. Ingersoll suppressed a smile. "And what did Miss Charman say to that?"

"She kept them in after school."

"Well, there now!" Mrs. Ingersoll smoothed back Laura's hair. "They got what they deserved and next time they'll know better."

"Oh, no, they won't! They're just mean, stupid boys and they laughed when Miss Charman said Joan of Arc was burned at the stake." Laura's lip trembled and she looked up at her mother. "Is it really true? Did they really kill her?"

Mrs. Ingersoll hesitated. "Well, yes, Laura, they did. But as Miss Charman said, Joan of Arc was a very brave woman and that's what you have to remember."

"Well, it's still nothing for those stupid boys to laugh about."

"No," Mrs. Ingersoll agreed, "it isn't. But it's nothing for you to cry about either." She reached in the bowl on the table and handed Laura a Gravenstein apple. "Now go out and play and forget all about Buster."

"And Willie too?"

Mrs. Ingersoll smiled. "Yes, and Willie too!"

Laura Ingersoll was born in Great Barrington, Mass. on September 13, 1775. The oldest of the four children of Thomas Ingersoll and his wife, Elizabeth Dewey, she spent her early years in Massachusetts, growing up amid the uncertainty of the American Revolution. Her mother died when Laura was eight and her father, who had fought on the side of the Thirteen Colonies during the war, twice remarried.

In 1795, at the invitation of Governor John Simcoe, a close family friend, Ingersoll moved with his family to Upper Canada and obtained a township grant on the Thames River in Oxford County. He went first to Queenston on the Niagara Peninsula and while waiting for his land to be surveyed, operated a tavern and became well known in the community. In 1796 he moved to his new farm (which was to become the site of the present day town of Ingersoll), christened the township Oxford-upon-Thames and soon had between 80 and 90 families living on his land.

The following year Laura, who had grown into an attractive and vibrant young woman, announced her engagement to a Queenston merchant by the name of James Secord. The two had met and fallen in love while the Ingersolls were living in Queenston and they were married in 1797.

Secord came from an old and established family. Records show that one of his forebears, the Marquis D'Secor, served early in the 14th century as a Marshal in the Household of King Louis X of France. A son of the Marquis disgraced the family by becoming a Protestant and passing his faith on to succeeding generations. During the persecution of the Huguenots in France in the 16th and 17th centuries, many of the D'Secors died at the stake for refusing to repudiate their

41

faith and the family estates at La Rochelle were confiscated.

The survivors somehow escaped the St. Bartholomew's Day Massacre of 1572 when thousands of Protestants were slaughtered in Paris and some fled to England where they started new lives. Eventually a handful of the members of this branch of the family immigrated to America and settled in New Jersey where they purchased large tracts of land and became prosperous lumbermen.

When the American Revolution broke out in 1776, the family divided, with those remaining loyal to Great Britain changing their name from D'Secor to the more anglicized form of Secord. One of these Secords became an officer in the loyalist Butler's Rangers and moved with his family to the Niagara district of Upper Canada in 1778. His youngest son, then five years old, went on nineteen years later to marry Laura Ingersoll.

After their wedding in 1797, James and Laura lived briefly in St. Davids before settling in nearby Queenston where James operated a store. He later took over a lumber business and joined the Lincoln Militia.

The relationship between James and Laura was a warm and loving one and Laura, despite her slender build and extremely delicate appearance, had seven children — five of them before the War of 1812. The early years of their marriage were quiet and uneventful. In fact, had the war not obtruded upon their lives, the name Secord would most likely have gone unrecorded in the annals of Canadian history.

But by early 1812, friction between the United States and Great Britain over a number of issues, including the persistence of the Americans in trading with France while Britain was embroiled in the Napoleonic Wars, had made war in North America inevitable. British seizures of American vessels to search for deserters exacerbated ill feeling in the United States and led to a growing desire on the part of many Americans to annex Canada.

By the time war was officially declared on June 18, 1812, most Canadians were prepared for a long ordeal. One who was taken by surprise, however, was James Secord, who had held the rank of captain in the Lincoln Militia and had resigned his commission over a disagreement with a superior officer. Nevertheless, when the call to arms came, Secord immediately rejoined and served as a sergeant in his old militia regiment, which was put under the command of Major General Sir Issac Brock.

In October, while Secord was away on military duty, a force of Americans invaded Queenston and spread through the village commandeering money and supplies and searching for weapons. As they neared the Secord house, Laura quickly gathered together a highly prized collection of Spanish doubloons and tossed them into a cauldron of boiling water, which hung on a crane over a blazing fire. She later discovered that in 1685, during the persecution that followed the repeal of the Edict of Nantes, which had granted religious toleration to French Protestants, one of her husband's ancestors had thrown a copy of the Bible into a milk churn to prevent it from being confiscated by troops searching the homes of known Protestants for proof of so-called unorthodoxy.

According to some sources, a second group of American soldiers subsequently stopped at the Secord house during the invasion of Queenston. One of this group supposedly told Laura that once Upper Canada had been overrun he would come back and claim the Secord property as his own. His arrogance infuriated Laura and she promptly told him that the only land he would ever get in Queenston would be a six foot grave. A few hours later two of the men returned and told Laura that her prediction had been accurate — the third man had been killed by a Canadian bullet.

In the meantime, while American soldiers were running freely through the streets of Queenston, Brock was preparing to launch a counteroffensive and on October 13, 1812 the Battle of Queenston Heights was fought in all its fury. It turned out to be one of the most decisive battles of the war and the British victory secured Upper Canada until the following spring. Brock was killed before the outcome of the battle was determined and James Secord was seriously wounded in both the leg and shoulder. He lay for hours on the battlefield, which was only a short distance from his home, until the last shots were fired and he was rescued by his wife.

The Americans drew back for the winter, but when spring came, they renewed their offensive and the situation in the Niagara district once again grew tense. Fort George, five miles north of Queenston, was captured and by June the Americans were imposing harsh restrictions on the people of Queenston and the surrounding district. The soldiers took full advantage of their new authority over the local population and walked unannounced into people's homes and demanded food and shelter.

On the evening of June 21, 1813, several officers forced their way into the Secord home in Queenston and ordered Laura to serve them dinner. As the evening progressed, the officers grew incautious and began discussing American plans to crush what remained of British resistance in the area.

At Beaver Dams a few miles to the west, a small outpost of British soldiers had been placed under the command of Lieutenant James FitzGibbon, a dashing young officer, 33 years old, who had earned his commission through distinguished service. The son of an Irish cottager, he had educated himself and acquired the manners of a gentleman.

If the Americans could surprise FitzGibbon at the remote two-storey stone house he was holed up in, they could open up the entire peninsula. Laura overheard the conversation and knew that unless FitzGibbon was warned, the whole area would remain at the mercy of the Americans for years to come. James was still recovering from his wounds and could not possibly make the trip. That left only Laura.

To go all the way by road was out of the question. It would expose her to the threat of being stopped by American patrols. Instead, she decided to take a circuitous and treacherous twenty mile route that would take her as far as St. Davids by road, through a swamp by Twelve Mile Creek, up the Escarpment and finally through the woods to the stone house where FitzGibbon was quartered.

Early the next morning, dressed in everyday clothing to avoid suspicion, she set out for St. Davids. Before she had reached her own gate, an American soldier spotted her and asked where she was going so early in the morning. With a story already planned, she told him that a cow had strayed from the barn and that she was trying to find it. The explanation seemed plausible enough and the soldier went about his business. She was stopped twice more before she reached St. Davids and both times she managed to get through by saying she was on her way to visit a brother who was sick and quite possibly dying.

When she finally arrived in St. Davids she went directly to the home of Elizabeth Secord, the widow of James' brother, Stephen. She rested there and told her sister-in-law her plan. According to some accounts, one of Elizabeth's daughters joined Laura for the next stage of her journey, going as far as Shipman's Corners (present day St. Catharines) before giving up in exhaustion. Whatever the case, at Shipman's Corners Laura turned off the road and entered the swamp. The worst part of her trip was now upon her.

Uncertain of the way, she decided to follow Twelve Mile Creek. Her clothes were quickly torn on the sharp burdocks and thorns and the damp bogs soon soaked her to the skin. Alone and unarmed she knew that if one of the wildcats or wolves that inhabited the area attacked her, she stood little chance of survival, but still she drove herself on, stopping only briefly to rest.

In the afternoon she heard the howling of a pack of wolves and for the first time, she panicked. However, the howls grew fainter as the pack moved away, and she continued on.

As darkness fell she realized the creek was taking her too far west and that she would have to cross it. Heavy rains had swollen it to twice its normal size and in her exhausted condition she knew she could not fight the swiftly flowing water. As she searched the bank for a place to cross, she spied a tree sprawled from one bank to the other and gingerly made her way across on that. Once on the other side she stopped to rest, then climbed the steep slope of the escarpment and left the swamp behind her.

Making her way through the thick undergrowth, she began to sense that she was being watched. With what little speed she could muster, she ran into a clearing and was immediately surrounded by a group of Caughnawaga Indians. For a moment she was paralyzed by fear, then summoning the last of her strength, she managed with great difficulty to make the chief understand where she was going and why it was so important she get there. The chief, who preferred the British to the Americans, admired her courage and ordered one of his men to take her to FitzGibbon.

An hour or so later, as the moon began to rise, Laura arrived at FitzGibbon's outpost, told him of the American plan to attack, and collapsed from exhaustion. FitzGibbon revived her and arranged for her to be taken to the nearby home of her friend, Miss Tourney. There Laura fell into a deep sleep. She returned to Queenston on June 24th, and until that time her husband, who had been forced to hide his anxiety for fear of arousing the suspicions of the American soldiers in the neighbourhood, had had no word from her.

The day Laura returned home, the Americans were ambushed near Beaver Dams by four hundred Indians loyal to the British and were quickly overpowered. FitzGibbon then accepted the surrender of the American force, which outnumbered his by almost nine to one.

In the official reports of the battle no mention was made of Laura's efforts and for years her role in the Beaver Dams incident was little known. However, in a letter dated May 11, 1827, FitzGibbon wrote:

"...on the 22d day of June 1813, Mrs. Secord, Wife of James Secord, Esq. ...came to me at Beaver Dam (sic) after SunSet, having come...by a circuitous route...and informed me that...a Detachment from the American Army then in Fort George would be sent out on the following morning (the 23rd.) for the purpose of Surprising and capturing a Detachment of the 49th Regt. then at the Beaver Dam (sic) under my command...

"The weather on the 22d. was very hot, and Mrs. Secord whose person was slight and delicate appeared to have been and no doubt was very much exhausted by the exertion She made in coming to me, and I have ever since held myself personally indebted to her for her conduct upon that occasion..."

The victory at Beaver Dams was an important one for the British. The Indian buildup that followed the battle intimidated the Americans and forced them to reevaluate their position. The war was not yet over, but the Americans knew that Canada would not give up without a fight.

46

FitzGibbon, who had been in Canada since 1802, went on to see action in other battles of the war and was promoted to the rank of captain, then colonel and finally, in 1822, assistant adjutant-general. During the rebellion led by William Lyon MacKenzie in 1837, he helped organize the defense of Toronto and in 1846 he returned to England where, in 1850, he was appointed a military knight of Windsor.

Fate did not treat Laura as kindly. Although the war ended in 1814 and the Americans withdrew from Canada, life for the Secords was never quite the same. James did not fully recover from the wounds he suffered at the Battle of Queenston Heights and for a long time he was unable to return to work. Two more children were born after the war and the small pension James received for his military service did little to meet the family's growing needs.

Finally, in 1828 he was appointed registrar of the Niagara Surrogate Court in nearby Chippawa. He sold the house in Queenston and moved his family to Chippawa early in the fall. Five years later he was appointed judge of the same court and in 1835 he became Chippawa's new collector of customs.

But as time passed, Laura, who usually preferred not to discuss the part she had played in thwarting the American capture of Beaver Dams, began to feel that her efforts were worthy of some form of recognition. In 1839 she wrote to government officials requesting that she be allowed to lease a ferry at Queenston on preferred terms. The request was denied and when she was left in financial straits by her husband's death in 1841, she applied unsuccessfully for a pension in recognition of her services to the country in 1813.

For awhile after that she supported herself by taking day students at her home in Chippawa. But she was by then almost 70 and soon gave it up. Finally, in 1860 Edward, Prince of Wales (later King Edward VII) paid a visit to Canada. During a brief stopover in Queenston, he was presented with a document by Laura, which recounted her wartime adventure. The Prince was intrigued by the story and after he returned to England he sent a gift of £100, which was presented to Laura by ten men who had been part of the Prince's entourage.

After that, interest in Laura's adventure began to

spread. The following year historian Benson Lossing put together a "Pictorial Field Book of the War of 1812." He contacted Laura and in a letter to him dated February 18, 1861 she gave him a brief outline of the events that led up to the Battle of Beaver Dams. Soon poems were written glorifying her deed and a play, "Laura Secord the Heroine of the War of 1812," was written by Sarah Anne Curzon, a leading Canadian literary figure of the 1880s and 1890s.

For many writers, imagination took up where fact left off and Laura was often (and it appears inaccurately) depicted as taking a cow with her on her trip to Beaver Dams to camouflage her true intent. When she spotted an American soldier on the road she supposedly milked the cow; then, when the soldier was out of sight, she let the animal go, entered the swamp and continued on to find FitzGibbon.

As a woman well past her 85th birthday, Laura basked in the new recognition. Her last years were spent quietly and peacefully and she died on October 17, 1868 at the age of 93.

MARY PICKFORD

The little girl who would one day grow up to become the world's first great international film star stood outside the flower shop on Queen Street in Toronto with a shiny penny clutched tightly in her fist.

Today was the day! She had made up her mind and now all she had to do was go through with it. She reached up, turned the door knob and entered the shop. The sweet fragrance of the flowers filled the air and she breathed in the perfume greedily.

"Well, hello there, Gladys Smith," the florist said as he looked up from the bouquet he was arranging. "I figured it was about time you paid me another visit." He put the last carnation in the vase, then walked over to the glass cooler. "What colour do you want today?"

Gladys peered in at the fresh bundles of tiny rosebuds. It was a hard decision. She pursed her lips. The white ones were pretty and so were the yellow, but the red ones were the best of all. "I think I'll take a red one." She gazed up at him hopefully. "That one in the back by the fern."

The florist reached in the cooler, picked out the rose and handed it to her with a flourish. "That will be one cent please, madam."

Gladys put the penny in his hand and drew the flower to her face. The petals were soft and velvety and the fragrance was absloutely glorious.

"All right, now," the florist said, "off you go. Maybe next week I'll have some peach ones." He turned back to the counter and began to pull some wilted roses from a display that he had taken from the window. One by one he dropped the faded blossoms into the waste basket.

Gladys squared her shoulders. This was the moment

she had been waiting for. Softly she moved forward and tugged on the florist's smock.

He looked down at her and put his hands on his hips. "You still here? I thought by now you'd be home putting that rose in water."

Gladys shook her head.

"Well then, what's the matter? Did you pick out the wrong one?"

"No-o-o," Gladys hestitated. "I was just wondering," she said timidly, "if maybe I could have one of those roses in the waste basket."

"They're dead!"

"Oh, that's all right."

The florist scratched his head. "Well, I don't know what you want it for," he said good-naturedly as he bent down and picked up an overblown pink rose, "but here — it's yours. Absolutely free!"

Gladys took it and thanked him, then turned and ran out the door. Now she could do it! She hurried around the corner and down the street to her home. Quietly, not to let anyone know she was back, she opened the door and tiptoed up the stairs. Alone in her room, she plucked one of the petals from the faded rose and put it in her mouth. It was as bitter as the medicine she had had to take the last time she was sick, but she closed her eyes, chewed it up and swallowed it. She knew that *somehow* the original beauty, colour and fragrance of the rose would one day become part of her. It was a ritual she would follow for weeks to come and one she would remember for the rest of her life.

Gladys Smith was born in Toronto, Ontario on April 9, 1893. The eldest of the three children of John Smith, a down-on-his-luck ship's purser, and his wife, Charlotte Mary Catherine Pickford Hennessey, Gladys spent her early years living in genteel poverty. Her father died when Gladys was four and to keep the family together her mother opened a penny candy counter in a grocery store.

But the income was not enough and Mrs. Smith soon turned her home at 211 University Avenue into a boarding house and began to take in sewing at night. In 1898 she rented a room to the stage manager of the Cummings Stock Company of Toronto. One day the new boarder asked Mrs. Smith if Gladys and her sister, Lottie, could appear in the schoolroom scene of a play he was producing entitled "The Silver King."

After much hesitation, Mrs. Smith agreed and Gladys, playing a little boy in the last act, was told to amuse herself quietly with a set of blocks and a toy horse at left center stage while the two stars engaged in an important piece of dialogue. Instead, Gladys built the blocks into a huge pyramid and knocked it down with the little horse.

The audience roared its approval but the stage manager, who was a born perfectionist, stood in the wings and fumed. When the curtain fell he explained to five year old Gladys the dishonour of stealing a scene, then softened his lecture by telling her that her bit of improvisation would remain, but that the blocks were to be knocked down at a point that would not detract from the dialogue.

Shortly after "The Silver King" ended its run in Toronto, Gladys developed pneumonia. It was one of several severe illnesses she had as a child — illnesses that ebbed her strength and permitted her to attend school for a total of six months in her entire life. Mrs. Smith, who had been taught by nuns, took over Gladys' education and when other parts followed the one Gladys had played in "The Silver King," began a rigorous program to train Gladys' memory.

In 1900 Gladys was engaged by the Valentine Stock Company of Toronto and was given a part in a play that was written and produced by the noted American dramatist, Hal Reid. Reid was so impressed by Gladys' performance that he promised to hire all four Smiths for the play's forthcoming Broadway run. However, he soon suffered a financial setback and was forced to sell the production rights to the play. When the company finally went on tour, the new management hired Lillian Gish to take over Gladys' role.

Then, a short time into the run, Gish was forced to withdraw and someone remembered the performance Gladys had given in Toronto. A wire was sent to Mrs. Smith requesting that Gladys be allowed to join the company in Buffalo and take up her old part. After careful consideration, Mrs. Smith agreed, but on the condition that she and her other two children also be given roles — she would not have the

51

family, which was a close one, broken up. In the end, the company gave in and the Smiths went to Buffalo, continued the tour, and arrived in New York for the 1901-02 season.

The following year Gladys (billed as Baby Gladys Smith) starred in the touring production of "The Fatal Wedding" and over the next few years she and the rest of the family travelled the length and breadth of the United States. Occasionally they took time off to visit family and friends in Toronto, but the visits were always of short duration. Charlotte Smith realized the possibilities that existed in the theatre and she believed the best hope for success lay in the United States.

In 1906 Gladys auditioned for a part on Broadway. She won over many other candidates, but was told by producer David Belasco that her name would have to be changed. Plucking bits and pieces from the Smith family tree, Belasco came up with the name, "Mary Pickford." The other Smiths liked the new surname and decided to adopt it as well, even going so far as to register the change with the Canadian government.

But a new name did not make a new beginning and the family continued to have its financial ups and downs. Finally, in 1909, Mrs. Smith (now Pickford) suggested that Gladys (now Mary) audition for a part in the motion pictures being produced at the Biograph Studio in New York. At that time actors who appeared in the recently developed "flickers" were regarded as outcasts by serious Broadway performers. However, the family needed the money and Mary, unwilling to disappoint her mother for whom she had a deep affection, agreed.

Her first film, "The Violin Maker of Cremona," led to many more, and in the years that followed she played scrubwomen and secretaries, sweethearts and servants in a variety of short one reel films that were turned out at the rate of two a week. Although her talent was largely underrated, audiences were entranced by her golden curls and girlishness. Her warm personality with its mixture of strength and vulnerability made her credible as a poor girl, a rich girl and anything in between. Money ceased to be a problem for the Pickfords and life became more pleasurable. Movies were in

52

mass production and their popularity with general audiences was soaring.

Although Mary was pleased with her new success, something was still missing in her life and on January 7, 1911 she married Owen Moore, an actor she had met on her first day at the Biograph Studio. Moore was ten years her senior and was the actor who had taught her how to make love on the screen. Despite her restrained style of acting, Mary lived her roles and she had fallen in love with Moore soon after she met him and acted with him. At first Mrs. Pickford had ignored the situation hoping Mary would lose interest in an older man. By the time she realized how serious the two really were, it was too late. Mary ignored her mother's order that she not see Moore outside the studio and clandestine meeting followed clandestine meeting until the two were finally married in secret. They kept the news to themselves for several months before breaking it to the mother of the bride.

Mrs. Pickford took the announcement better than Mary had expected, but as it turned out, it really didn't matter. Cracks in the marriage soon began to surface and the newlyweds were far from happy. Moore resented Mary's family, her growing fame and burgeoning paycheque and didn't know how to deal with it.

For her part, Mary threw herself into her work and returned to live theater before starring in 1914 in a new five reel film, "Tess of the Storm Country." It was during the release of this film that she was dubbed "America's Sweetheart." Her success was so great that by 1915 she was earning $4,000 weekly against 50% of the total profits of Famous Players, the studio she was then associated with, and together with her mother she was carefully nurturing her growing fortune. By 1918 she was established as an independent producer and was earning a basic salary of $675,000 a year against 50% of the gross receipts of her films. Yet, despite the successes in her professional life, her personal life was still far from happy.

Three years earlier, Mary and Owen, who had broken up and temporarily reconciled, had attended a party where they had met Douglas Fairbanks, the dashing swashbuckler of the silver screen, and his wife, Beth. At the time, the meeting of Hollywood's two greatest stars had meant nothing to either one, but eventually it would change the course of both their lives.

Fairbanks began to see a great deal of Mary. The two fell in love and in March, 1919 Fairbanks was divorced by his wife. Although Mary had by that time left Owen for good, she hesitated about seeking her own divorce for fear the stigma would ruin her career. In the end, however, her love for Fairbanks (who, like Moore, was ten years her senior) won out and her divorce was granted on March 2, 1920.

Four weeks later she and Fairbanks were married in Los Angeles. After the wedding supper they went to Pickfair, the white country house in Beverly Hills that Fairbanks presented to Mary as a wedding gift. News of their marriage attracted world wide attention. Hollywood's two greatest stars had united to form their own constellation. The fans loved it and the glory of their marriage soon laid to rest the disgrace of their divorces. Wherever they went, both in North America and Europe, they were met by crowds clamouring for autographs.

Mary was happier than she had ever been before. For years she had been extremely lonely. She did not make friends easily and had almost no women friends except for her mother. She wanted above all to be loved and approved of and Fairbanks gave her the emotional support she needed. For the first eight years of their marriage the two were inseparable. They travelled together, visiting the world's most glamorous cities, and when they were home, Pickfair became the center of the Hollywood social whirl. On weekends and between breaks in shooting, they entertained so elegantly and so lavishly that their parties became legendary. Royalty, intellectuals and celebrities of every description paid visits to Pickfair while an admiring (and envious) world looked on.

But even with the hectic schedule of her new life, Mary did not forget her mother. Charlotte Pickford, who had long since devoted herself to looking after Mary, Mary's career and Mary's money, continued to be Mary's closest friend and greatest confidante.

Roots were important to Mary and her mother was the most important root of all. But she was not the *only* root. National loyalties were also important to her and she never forgot the fact that by birth she was a Canadian. All her life she had retained her Canadian citizenship and she had visited Toronto many times. However, at the height of her stardom, she received notice that because she was a long time resident of the United States and because she earned her living in her place of residence, she would have to renounce her Canadian citizenship and take out American papers. The news infuriated Mary and she decided to fight. In the end she was successful and in 1924 she returned to Toronto on a much heralded visit and received an enormous welcome.

But life was not always fanfare and glory. The days Mary spent at the studio were long and arduous. She was up at five and at the studio by six. The next three hours were spent washing and setting her hair and making up her face. In high humidity shooting would have to stop so her drooping curls could be reset in rags. Usually her workday did not end until eight or nine p.m. and most nights she fell into bed exhausted.

Yet Mary, together with other Hollywood luminaries, knew that the long hours and harried schedules were doing something for the industry — an industry that was growing every year. On May 4, 1927, to ensure the future excellence of motion pictures and to give cohesion to the industry, thirty-six of the biggest names in Hollywood, including Mary and Douglas, banded together to form the Academy of Motion Picture Arts and Sciences.

It was during this stage of her life that Mary began buying up as many of her old negatives as she could (including eighty Biograph shorts) to prevent the possibility of their ever being reissued. She was convinced that future generations would laugh at the quality of the films turned out during Hollywood's infancy and for a long time she actually planned to have the negatives destroyed after her death.

To Mary at the age of 35, the past looked better than the future and she soon found herself at a crossroad. Sound had begun to revolutionize the motion picture industry and Mary knew that in order to maintain her status as Hollywood's foremost star, she would have to adapt to the new technology. But before she had time to plan her first "talkie," she was hit by a severe blow that would eventually kill her enthusiasm for acting.

Her mother, who had always been the most important person in Mary's life and who had been battling cancer for three years, suddenly took a turn for the worse. For the last eighteen months of Charlotte's life, Mary and Douglas lived with her and took care of her. The closeness between Mary and her mother intensified as never before and when Charlotte finally died on March 21, 1928, Mary was inconsolable.

After several weeks of deep mourning she decided the best way to pull herself together was to take the plunge into sound. She bought the rights to the highly successful Broadway play, "Coquette," and when the film version was released in April, 1929 Mary, in the starring role, received overwhelming critical acclaim. She was awarded the Academy of Motion Picture Arts and Sciences Best Actress Award for 1929 and it looked as though she had made the transition to sound with flying colours.

But it was not to be. Later that year she was persuaded to give audiences something they had long been waiting for — a film that co-starred her with Douglas Fairbanks. From the first day of shooting Mary knew the picture was doomed, and despite the cast, the production of "The Taming of the Shrew" fell flat. Although many critics praised it, audiences did not and Mary readily admitted that her performance was one of the worst of her career. Her drive was gone.

Two more sound pictures, disappointing to both Mary and her fans, followed in 1931 and 1932 and late in 1932, without making a formal announcement, Mary decided to retire from the screen. She later explained herself by saying she wanted to quit while she was still at the top, before someone came along and asked her to step down.

During the same time she was suffering the death throes of her career, Mary began to experience a change in her relationship with Fairbanks. His image had always been one of dynamism and youthful vitality and somehow he could not come to grips with the fact that as a man well past 40 he had all but outlived his glory.

He became increasingly impatient and restless and his moods eventually began to affect both his work and his relationship with Mary. Separations, which had been unheard of during the early years of the Fairbanks' marriage, became commonplace and Douglas began seeing other women. For four years — from 1930 to 1934 — the press speculated on the marital difficulties brewing at Pickfair and for four years Mary said nothing. Then, on January 10, 1935, when she could tolerate Fairbanks' extramarital affairs no longer, she filed for divorce.

With stardom and her marriage behind her, she produced a number of films, then took up writing (her 1935 novel *The Demi-Widow* sold well), did a weekly radio show and appeared in a short run of the stage version of "Coquette."

On June 26, 1937 she and Buddy Rogers, a band leader and ex-actor eleven years Mary's junior who had first met Mary during the filming of "My Best Girl" in 1927, were married in Los Angeles. After much deliberation the newly weds decided to ignore the lingering spectre of Douglas Fairbanks and live at Mary's beloved Pickfair.

In 1943, when Mary was 51 and Rogers 40, they adopted a six year old boy and in 1944 a six month old girl. Although the first years of parenthood were happy ones, the experience gradually went sour and after the children turned 21, Mary, while providing for them financially, refused to have anything more to do with them.

Throughout the 1950s she became active in charities and in the early 60s received honourary degrees from a number of American colleges. In 1963 she took her last trip to Toronto where she presented a huge tapestry handcrafted by Queen Mary, Consort of King George V, to a Toronto museum.

As the years passed she became increasingly reclusive, often refusing to leave her bed. She withdrew from public life in 1966 and began to live in seclusion at Pickfair with Buddy, her memories and a few loyal staff members.

In 1970 she donated 51 of her Biograph shorts to the American Film Institute Collection in the Library of Congress. Six years later she appeared before cameras at Pickfair to accept an honourary award "in recognition of her unique contribution to the film industry and the development of film as an artistic medium" from the Academy of Motion Picture Arts and Sciences. It was the world's last glimpse of its first great star.

On Friday, May 25, 1979 Mary suffered a cerebral

hemorrhage and was rushed by ambulance from Pickfair to Santa Monic Hospital, where she died on May 29th at the age of 86.

Emily Carr and her pet bob-tail English sheep-dogs in her garden (Public Archives of Canada — C 20368)

Big Eagle, Skidigate, B.C. by Emily Carr (Art Gallery of Greater Victoria. Photo: Trevor Mills)

E. Pauline Johnson — Tekahionwake (Public Archives of
Canada — PA 111473)

"AND HE SAID 'FIGHT ON'."

(Tennyson)

Time, and its ally, Dark Disarmament
Have compassed me about,
Have massed their armies, and on battle bent
My forces put to rout,
But though I fight alone, and fall, and die,
Talk terms of Peace? Not I.

They war upon my fortress, and their guns,
Are shattering its walls,
My army plays the cowards' part and runs
Pierced by a thousand balls,
They call for my surrender, I reply
"Give quarter now? Not I."

They've shot my flag to ribbons, but in rents
It floats above the height.
Their Ensign shall not crown my battlements
While I can stand and fight.
I fling defiance at them as I cry
"Capitulate? Not I."

E. PAULINE JOHNSON
— Tekahionwake

3

Maude Abbott (Public Archives of Canada — C 9479)

Laura Secord (Ontario Archives)

Mary Pickford (Public Archives of Canada — C 52029)

Judy LaMarsh (Public Archives of Canada — PA 108053)

Karen Kain in the National Ballet of Canada production of
"Don Juan." (Public Archives of Canada — PA 133983)

L. M. Montgomery (Public Archives of Canada — C 11299)

Mazo de la Roche (Public Archives of Canada — C5482)

Barbara Ann Scott doing a "Stag Jump." (Public Archives of Canada — PA 112691)

JUDY LAMARSH

The gangly fourteen year old sat cross-legged on the floor, her round face drawn in a sullen frown. Why hadn't she said no? Words whirled by in a dizzying blur as she flipped angrily through the pages of a movie magazine. It was so degrading and there wasn't a thing in the world she could do about it.

Suddenly, far away, a door slammed and she was jarred back to the present. Footsteps clicked on the oak floor. With a rush of panic she blinked back the tears and stared intently at the magazine.

"Was that the phone I heard a little while ago, Judy?" her mother asked as she came into the living room with a vase full of flowers.

Judy burrowed her face deeper in the magazine and nodded.

"Well — who was it?"

"*Who* was it? What you really mean is *what* was it!" She drew her knees to her chin and flipped the page. "Old Lady Killer himself decided to make my whole day and do some slumming." She scowled darkly at a picture of Clark Gable.

"What on *earth* are you talking about?"

Judy's face twisted in a look of long-suffering pain. She wished they could just drop it. "Nothing, okay? Just nothing!"

"Now, look here! I want to know what you're talking about and I want to know right this minute."

Judy threw the magazine down and rose quickly to her feet. "Oh — it's that stupid dance."

"You mean the one Friday night?"

Judy nodded.

"Weren't you invited?"

"Oh, I was invited all right! But it certainly wasn't by

your average captain of the football team." She threw back her head and stared wide-eyed at the ceiling. "You know, for once in my life I'd like to be the one a guy asked first. Being Pee Wee Logan's third choice isn't exactly what I call flattering!"

"You're always invited to the dances, Judy."

"Invited? It seems to me more like I'm asked by default."

"You're not being fair. You're popular and you know it!"

Judy winced. "Yeah? Well there's more to my idea of popularity than being elected to the students' council. For once — just once — I'd like to be somebody's first choice!"

Julia Verlyn LaMarsh was born in Chatham, Ontario on December 20, 1924. Her father, Wilfred LaMarsh, was a well respected criminal lawyer and her mother, Rhoda, was a gifted painter.

The second of three children, Judy grew up in Chatham and Niagara Falls, Ontario where she enjoyed all the advantages of a middle class upbringing. Once, in speaking of her childhood, she recalled the time when, as a very little girl she developed a mania for collecting pictures of brides. The reason for her passion eluded the adult Judy who vehemently denied the suggestion she had ever wanted to be a bride herself.

As she passed from childhood into adolescence, Judy turned her attention from weddings and brides to movie magazines and boys. Like most girls her age, she read *Photoplay* omnivorously and regarded boys as a vital necessity. Without boys there were no invitations to dances and without invitations Judy's self-esteem withered.

At school Judy was only mediocre. She preferred sports and drama to cramming for exams, and in her spare time she dabbled in school politics. Her parents, both ardent Liberals, instilled in her at an early age the belief that politics was everyone's business and that despite its disappointments, it offered moments of great excitement.

The constant talk fascinated Judy and in high school she launched her first campaign, winning a seat on the students' council. The thrill of holding elected office sharpened her interest in politics, but the idea of serving as a politician did not then interest her. Careerwise her sights were
60

set on something different.

All her life she had dreamed of becoming a lawyer and the thought of not being allowed to go on to university had never really occurred to her. In 1942, during her last year of high school, she told her parents her plans and began to pick out a college.

Then, came the painful truth. Her father could only afford to send one child to university and he felt that Judy's brother, who was two years younger, should be the one to go. It was a bitter blow and one that Judy would long remember.

Angry and hurt, and determined to strike out on her own, she went to the nearest recruiting office of the Women's Division of the Royal Canadian Air Force and tried to enlist. When she was turned down because of her poor eyesight, she enrolled half-heartedly in Hamilton Normal School and graduated a year later with a primary teaching certificate. But teaching five year olds did not appeal to Judy and at the age of eighteen she joined the Canadian Women's Army Corps.

After basic training she took a special drafting course in Toronto and was posted to Halifax for a year with the Royal Canadian Engineers before being transferred to Vancouver in 1944 to study Japanese. Early in 1945 she was sent to Washington, D.C. to serve with a special multinational unit at the U.S. Pacific Military Intelligence Research Station translating documents seized from the Japanese.

When the war finally ended in 1945 she served with the Army for another year before resigning and enrolling at government expense in Victoria College at the University of Toronto. During the brief thirteen months it took her to earn her Bachelor of Arts Degree, she joined the Young Liberal Club and became heavily involved in school politics.

In 1947 she went on to Osgoode Hall Law School and three years later was called to the Bar of Ontario. In 1950 she went into partnership with her father in Niagara Falls and, once established in her practice, began to devote more of her time to politics.

Before her father died in 1957 she was appointed to the executive of a number of Liberal organizations and was offered the party's nomination for the riding of Niagara Falls in the upcoming provincial election. The idea of serving in the

Legislature appealed to Judy and for a time she seriously considered running for office. Then, realizing anti-Liberal sentiment in the riding would make her little more than a sacrificial lamb, she bowed out.

When the next provincial nominating meeting for Niagara Falls was held in 1959, the political climate had changed and Judy, who was then President of the Ontario Women's Liberal Association and more confident of her chances, offered herself as a candidate. Her earlier retreat had not been forgotten and she was soundly defeated.

However, as President of the Ontario Women's Liberal Association, she continued to keep a high profile and when the federal member for Niagara Falls died in 1960, she decided to seek the Liberal nomination.

This time she was successful. But she still faced an uphill struggle. Liberal popularity was at an unprecedented low and the New Democratic Party was determined to take the riding.

It looked like a long campaign. Then, to everyone's surprise, a Buffalo television station offered to stage a live three candidate debate. All parties agreed and a mutually convenient evening was chosen. As the cameras began to roll, the New Democratic candidate, determined to keep his name and that of his party in full view of the audience, pulled out his campaign pamphlet and propped it up in front of him. Infuriated, Judy reached over, grabbed the pamphlet, threw it on the floor and acidly inquired if the only way he could remember his platform was to have it written out in black and white. Silence descended upon the studio. In the control booth, Judy's campaign manager blanched. Whatever chance she had had of winning he felt had just wafted to the studio floor.

But he was wrong. Later that evening at a political rally in Niagara Falls, Judy found her constituents applauding her outspokenness and vigour. She went on to win the election by 5,000 votes and in the three elections that followed over the next five years she eventually doubled that margin.

But politics offers little time to savour victory. Two weeks after the 1960 by-election Parliament reconvened. No one — not a Liberal M.P. nor a worker for the Liberal Party —

contacted Judy to advise her on the procedure to follow her first day in the House. Finally, totally at a loss, Judy called Mary Macdonald, Opposition Leader Lester Pearson's executive assistant, to find out what to expect. Macdonald told Judy she would be led down the center aisle of the House of Commons and introduced to the Speaker by the Party Leader. She added that it was customary for new members to appear in evening dress. The idea of parading down the aisle dressed up like a teen-ager on the way to her first prom disgusted Judy and with her usual self-assurance she decided to wear a plain black street length dress. She later discovered that the only woman to wear an evening gown in the House of Commons in the last century had been Queen Elizabeth II when she officiated at the opening of Parliament in 1958. From that time on, Judy took advice from the so-called experts with a grain of salt.

Her first days in Ottawa were not what she had expected. No one came forward to introduce himself and no one offered suggestions on how to go about setting up her office. In the midst of her isolation she found that most of the Liberal members were still wallowing in the defeat Diefenbaker had dumped on them in 1958 and had no idea of the growing public disillusionment with the Conservative government.

For the first few weeks she sat alone with her hands folded, unable to do anything but watch and listen. Given no assignment and no instructions, she felt totally useless. Finally, the prevailing Opposition attitude of despair and depression became too much for her and she began to launch her own attack against the Diefenbaker administration.

The tough, abrasive politician who would soon become the darling of political cartoonists had begun to make her mark. Gradually Liberal M.P.s started to take notice of her and as jobs cropped up no one else wanted, they were dropped on her doorstep.

One day Lester Pearson threw his arm around Judy's shoulders and commended her on the way she had conducted herself during a parliamentary sitting. Professionally, she had arrived. But socially, she was still lost in the wilderness.

Male politicians continued to feel uncomfortable with her outside the house and their wives, unaccustomed to female she had little to fall back on. Living for years in the male dominated world of law, she had made few close female friends.

Then, in 1963, her life took a new direction and for a time she was too busy to reflect upon her loneliness. The Liberals were returned to power and with the influx of new blood, Judy was appointed to the Ministry of Health and Welfare. With eighteen years of service to the Liberal Party behind her, she felt it was nothing less than she deserved.

At the first meeting of her new cabinet, Pearson told his ministers to reorganize their departments immediately. Judy needed no further urging. Honest and fearless, with a deep-rooted enthusiasm for politics and unwavering loyalty to the Liberal Party, she was soon at work studying proposals for a new national contributory pension plan.

A few months later, with the plan taking shape, the Canadian insurance industry began to voice fears about the effect government intervention would have on the industry's lucrative company pension plan market. After weeks of bitter haggling, Judy was finally able to silence the opposition and late in 1964 she introduced the Canada Pension Plan Bill to the House of Commons. The slow passage of the legislation frustrated and disgusted her and her frequent outbursts of temper soon earned her a reputation as an obstinate street fighter.

The press hounded her night and day. As the only woman in the Pearson cabinet and the most colourful member of the House everything she did was news. Her explosive temper, combined with her unfortunate manner of wearing her emotions on her sleeve, made her a perfect target for criticism and scorn and a day rarely went by without her name being featured on the evening news.

Even her personal life was a matter of widespread interest. Once engaged to a naval officer for an ill-fated three days during her time at Osgoode Hall Law School, Judy made no secret of the fact she was fond of the opposite sex. But she steadfastly maintained she had never expected her life to revolve around marriage and motherhood. In speaking of her personal life to a reporter in 1964 she said she felt it would be unfair for her to marry and expect her husband to sit at home M.P.s, eyed her with suspicion. She was lonely and hurt and
64

while she attended a never ending round of cabinet meetings.

Longtime friend and political colleague Paul Hellyer saw the matter differently. Describing Judy as soft and feminine beneath her tough exterior, he said he felt that deep down she would have liked nothing better than to marry and raise a family.

Certainly there was little time during her years as Minister of Health and Welfare to devote to her personal life. No sooner had the Canada Pension Plan Bill been tabled than she was busy drawing up the framework for a national prepaid health insurance plan.

However, before the plan could be presented to Parliament, the government was defeated and Canadians once again faced a general election. When it was all over, the Liberals were returned to power, and Judy, much against her will, was appointed Secretary of State with the responsibility for organizing Canada's centennial celebration.

As plans for the festivities progressed, no one in Ottawa knew whether Canadians would take part in the celebration or ignore it. In the end, the gamble paid off. From the Centennial Caravan and Centennial Train to Expo and the Royal Tour, everything went off better than expected. The year was a success and full credit rested with Judy.

But in politics success is at best ephemeral. Dogging Judy's footsteps during her years as Secretary of State was the troublesome C.B.C. It's rapid growth and insatiable appetite for taxpayers' dollars had made it the bête noire of thousands of Canadians.

Taking the situation firmly in hand, Judy tabled a new Broadcasting Act and initiated internal reform in the Crown Corporation. But the wrangling in Parliament over the bill in general and the C.B.C. in particular soon began to wear on Judy's patience.

She was tired of fighting and fed up with the loneliness and criticism. In October, 1966 she told Pearson she had had enough. She didn't know whether to leave then and give someone else a chance to take over responsibility for the Centennial or else wait until the celebration was over and then resign. When Pearson told her he was retiring at the end of 1967, Judy decided to time her announcement with his.

65

In the end, things didn't quite work out that way. Pearson resigned earlier than he had planned and a leadership convention was scheduled for early in 1968. For a time, Judy considered running for the position herself. Although she still intended to stand by her decision to leave public life, she thought it was important that a creditable woman candidate enter the race. However, when she considered the time and money involved in staging a worthwhile campaign and the disinterest of the party in seeing a woman run, she dropped the idea and on April 10, 1968 she officially tendered her resignation.

The pressure was off. But before the memories dimmed, she decided to put her rare talent for saying exactly what she thought to use and she immediately began to work on a book. When *Memoirs of a Bird in a Gilded Cage*, with its explosive and often indiscreet account of the behind the scene dealings of the Liberal Party first appeared in book stores early in 1969, it became an overnight sensation.

Her new found celebrity appealed to Judy and she found herself enjoying life again. Job offers poured in and over the next few years she hosted a television show in Ottawa, had her own openline radio program in Vancouver and taught law at Osgoode Hall.

In 1974 she considered running for reelection in Niagara Falls, but dropped the idea when Liberal Leader Pierre Trudeau refused to guarantee her a place in his cabinet.

As the years passed, she went on the speaking circuit, reestablished her law practice, accepted a position on the board of directors of the Unity Bank, wrote a weekly column for the *Toronto Sun* and was named to head the Royal Commission on Violence in the Communication Industry. In 1979 she published her first novel, *A Very Political Lady* and followed it up in 1980 with *A Right Honourable Lady*.

As time dulled the impact of her days in politics, Judy's personality began to soften. Her basic toughness remained intact but she became less angry — less tense. Her uncompromising honesty and complete lack of pretense made her a respected political critic and her irreverent, often self-effacing humour continued to endear her to Canadians. Once, during a centennial visit to the Northwest Territories, she introduced herself to a group of Inuit by poking at her ample hips and laughing: "See, I brought my own supply of blubber!"

In her role as a private citizen, Judy found the satisfaction and contentment that had so long been missing. Her life was full and busy and she was happy viewing politics as an observer and not as a participant. Her greatest ambition was to write a sequel to *Memoirs of a Bird in a Gilded Gage* that would expose even more of the workings of the political system in Canada.

Then, in 1979, she found out she had cancer. After an operation to remove her gall bladder, doctors gave her three months to a year to live. Sapped of energy, her weight dropping drastically, Judy fought with characteristic ferocity. Yet, despite the help of a small circle of friends and the concern of former colleagues and constituents, she faced her last days alone.

When she was awarded the Order of Canada in her sick bed, she dismissed it as an afterthought and let fly with a customary broadside, questioning the significance of the award and denouncing as fools many of its earlier recipients.

As the disease ran its course, the pain became intolerable. Finally, on the afternoon of October 24, 1980 she made her last decision. "Okay," she told the doctors, "that's it. No more medication." She died three days later on October 27th at the age of fifty-five.

KAREN KAIN

As the last strains of the orchestra drifted softly through the auditorium, the ballerina floated across the stage and fluttered gracefully into the arms of Rudolf Nureyev. For a moment the audience sat transfixed.

Twelve year old Karen Kain edged forward in her seat. Within seconds the houselights would blaze and Maple Leaf Gardens would resound with applause. It was now or never!

Sidling into the aisle, scarcely daring to breathe for fear someone from the National Ballet School would see her, she turned towards the stage for one last glimpse of Rudolf Nureyev. As she did, the audience exploded and Nureyev was bathed in a crescendoing wave of rapturous applause.

With a tingle of excitement racing along her spine, Karen scurried up the aisle and into the main concourse. If only her school uniform didn't make her so conspicuous.

A few moments later, as she threaded her way through the maze of corridors, she heard the first rumble of footsteps. The crowd was on its way. Soon there would be a swarm of people trying to get backstage. If she positioned herself properly, she would be carried along with the crush and no one would notice her.

Rushing into the hallway that led to the wings, she planted herself firmly in the center of the floor and prepared for the onslaught. Within seconds she was lost in a forest of jostling humanity.

As the crowd pushed its way back toward the dressing rooms, Karen began to panic. Unable to see where she was going, she fought her way to the edge of the swarm and grabbed hold of a wooden panel. For a moment she lost her bearings. Then, looking up, she realized the panel was a piece of scenery. She was finally backstage!

Before she could decide upon the most likely way of finding Nureyev's dressing room, a shout echoed through the hallway and with a shudder the crowd began to move back the way it had come. Karen ducked down behind an artificial fir tree. Police, deaf to pleas the fans be allowed to catch just a glimpse of Nureyev, quickly cleared the area.

Huddled safely behind the props, Karen watched until the last policeman had followed the crowd around the corner. Now was her opportunity. Tiptoeing along the suddenly quiet corridor, she hoped against hope that she would find Nureyev before someone found her.

Then she saw it — the door with the name "Nureyev" emblazoned brightly in gold. Without waiting to knock, she turned the handle and rushed eagerly in.

There at his mirror, removing his makeup, sat Rudolf Nureyev. Karen stared at him blushingly. Without a word, she dug into her pocket and pulled out a paper. Thrusting it at him, she noticed the beads of sweat still glimmering on his forehead. It was a moment she would never forget.

Gently, Nureyev took the paper, signed it, and handed it back to her. Karen looked at him adoringly, muttered a few incoherent words of thanks, then turned and ran back into the corridor. She had done it! She had actually done it! They could punish her from now until Christmas for leaving the group, she didn't care. She had been face to face with Rudolf Nureyev and that was all that really mattered.

When Karen Kain was born in Hamilton, Ontario on March 28, 1951, there was nothing in her family background to indicate that she was destined for stardom. Her father, Charles, was an electrical engineer, and her mother, Winifred, was a suburban housewife.

The only thing that made Karen stand out was her great imagination. Although shy around strangers, she was often a ringleader with those she knew and as the eldest of four children, she organized her brother's and sisters' playtime, peppering their games with liberal doses of make-believe.

At school she used to round up her friends at recess and get them to act out scenes from books and stories. One of her favourites was "Robin Hood." With a wave of her wand, she transformed the fields around the school into Sherwood

69

Forest and turned her friends into Merry Men. She only insisted upon one thing — that the part of Maid Marian always be hers.

When her family moved from Hamilton to nearby Ancaster, Karen discovered a whole new world. The basement of the Kains' new house abounded with plumbing and Karen used to dangle from pipes in the ceiling, pretending she was a gymnast.

A few years later, as a special treat, her parents took her to Hamilton to see the world famous ballerina, Celia Franca, in a production of "Giselle." From that moment on, Karen was hooked — not on the dancing, on the costumes and music.

Soon after, she started to take ballet lessons from a neighbour in Ancaster. The costume she had to wear did not quite live up to her memories of the costumes she had seen in "Giselle." Instead of a flowing peasant dress, she wore green tights and a green sweater with a green ribbon in her hair. The outfit humiliated Karen and she used to run to her lessons, lurking behind trees, so no one would see her.

Her first exercises were done to the strains of one piece of music: "The Tennessee Waltz." Although the song quickly palled on Karen, she did not let the repetition dampen her enthusiasm. She enjoyed music as much as she did dancing, and at home she began to play records and dance by herself in the basement just for the pleasure of it.

In 1961 the Kains sold their house in Ancaster and moved to Mississauga. The promise Karen had shown in her first ballet lessons continued, and in 1962 she auditioned for the National Ballet School in Toronto. Betty Oliphant, principal of the school, recognized Karen's talent and accepted her at once.

Leaving home at the age of eleven to attend the National Ballet's boarding school in Toronto was extremely difficult for Karen. She was so dependent upon her mother that she couldn't even put her hair in a ponytail. But she wanted more than anything else in the world to become a ballerina and she was prepared to face the hardships.

Unfortunately, she was too young to foresee the dedication and discipline it would require to achieve her ambition and too naive to recognize the effect the self-sacrifice would have on the future course of her life. Her parents wanted what was best for her and were ambivalent about the entire situation. Her mother was concerned about the rigours and strain the school would impose and her father was concerned that she would not receive a sound enough academic education to prepare her for college. Eventually the doubts were cast aside and late in 1962 Karen left for Toronto.

Right from the beginning the transition from day school to boarding school took its toll. She was often lonely and homesick and she felt strange in her new surroundings. Betty Oliphant took pity on her and paid a great deal of attention to her, which Karen loved, but which made her very unpopular with the other students.

For weeks she cried herself to sleep, unable to come to grips with the fact she was so disliked. Gradually, however, the hostility of the other students wore off and Karen settled into a new routine.

As the years passed, she alternated between periods of docility and rebelliousness that made her personality difficult for her teachers to evaluate. Often, in headstrong moments, she disregarded the rules of the school, and on at least four occasions would have been expelled had Mrs. Oliphant not considered her talent too valuable to be wasted.

One of Karen's biggest problems was animals. She loved them and could see no harm in keeping them in her room. Once, while she was still quite new at the school, she smuggled a baby pigeon into her room and kept it alive for two weeks before it was finally discovered.

As puberty set in, Karen began to develop a new series of problems that made her fondness of animals pale in comparison. She became tall and overweight and her teeth started to be a source of real worry. More than protuberant, they had begun to stick straight out. Braces alone were not enough. She was forced to wear a metal retainer that encircled her entire head.

Her life became one unending misery. Bouts of homesickness once again plagued her and she worried constantly about her weight and teeth. In the midst of all this turmoil, however, she realized that not only did she love ballet, she was addicted to it.

She began to drive herself relentlessly and between 1964 and 1969 she won scholarships to continue her training from the Canada Council, the Ontario Arts Foundation, and the Ford Motor Company of Canada. The physical discomfort that goes hand in hand with ballet became an integral part of her life. Constant repetition of drills and exercises designed to hone her body to a state of fitness that would rival any athlete, was demanding and exhausting. But even chafing her feet until they bled and subjecting her legs and ankles to inhuman stress was not enough. She had to learn to do it with grace and poise — to make pirouetting en pointe look as natural as walking in a pair of slippers.

The demands were incessant and excruciating, but if she wanted to be a ballerina, they were also inescapable. Only by constant practice could she keep herself in peak condition — only through total dedication could she maintain the discipline to put her body through the torture of doing things it did not want to do. There was no time for outside interference; no time for distraction of any kind, and Karen was a stern taskmaster.

In the end, the effort paid off. She graduated in 1969 with an 89% academic average and was immediately accepted into the National Ballet of Canada's corps de ballet. A year later Peter Wright of the Royal Ballet saw her dance and chose her for the lead in his production of "The Mirror Walkers." Her performance attracted such attention that she was soon after named one of the National Ballet's five principal female dancers. She was on her way.

Exercising rigid authority over her life, she continued the compulsory daily exercise classes and worked six or more hours a day, six days a week. Her drive was insatiable and in 1971 she was given the leading role in the classic masterpiece, "Swan Lake."

The production opened its U.S. tour to glowing reviews and it seemed Karen had everything she had always wanted. Then, in the series of one-night stands that followed, she came face to face with her old nemesis: homesickness. She hated the nomadic existence and for a time seriously considered giving up her entire career. But her intrinsic love of dancing and the mounting recognition of her talent drove her on. She became the star attraction of the National Ballet and her skill improved with every performance.

To attract international attention for both itself and its new star, the National Ballet offered a lucrative contract to one of the most talented male dancers of all time — Rudolf Nureyev. Nureyev accepted the proposal and all at once the directors of the National Ballet found themselves in the unenviable position of having to provide him with a suitable leading lady. For a time, they let the matter ride.

Then, when Nureyev finally arrived in Canada, he solved the problem himself. Looking over the troupe, appraising its strengths and weaknesses, he suddenly noticed Karen Kain. Mechanically and technically, he felt she was superb. She had the suppleness and lucidity that marked her a star and her athletic ability and sense of balance and equilibrium, made her a choreographer's dream.

For Karen the prospect of dancing with Nureyev was both thrilling and terrifying. No longer a little girl skulking through the corridors of Maple Leaf Gardens, she realized that if she performed well, her future was made, and if she performed badly, it was all but ruined.

Up until her first rehersal with Rudolf Nureyev, Karen had been more comfortable with technique in dancing than with dramatic interpretation. Despite the guidance of her coaches at the national ballet, she could not put the feeling into her dancing that she knew she should. A very private person, she found it difficult to bare her emotions.

With Nureyev she lost her inhibitions and expanded her horizons. No longer caught up solely in technique, she found new courage and dimension and began to experience the thrill of dancing for the sake of dancing. What was more, she became an accomplished actress with a burning desire to give the best characterization and interpretation possible to her roles while still remaining sincere and unaffected.

In 1973 the National Ballet of Canada, with Rudolf Nureyev as guest dancer, appeared at the Metropolitan Opera House in New York to rave reviews. Surpassing even Nureyev, Karen, as the leading lady in "Swan Lake," earned the greatest accolades. Caught up in the drama, she had *become* the Swan Queen and had forgotten about whether she was dancing correctly. From that night on, she was not merely a dancer, but an artist as well.

The success of the New York run riveted critical attention on both the National Ballet and Karen Kain, and in the months that followed, Karen debuted as the female lead in both "The Sleeping Beauty" and "Giselle."

That same year she went to Moscow to take part in the International Ballet Competition. Partnered with Frank Augustyn of the National Ballet, she found the trip a grueling and frustrating experience. She abhorred the idea of reducing ballet to a personal confrontation among peers and the unfamiliar stages and difficult practice conditions put her increasingly on edge.

During the time she was in the Soviet Union she lost fifteen pounds and began to fear that she would not have enough stamina to perform in the competition. In the end, her apprehensions proved groundless. Not only did she and Augustyn advance into the finals of the pas de deux (dance for two performers) against forty other couples, Karen also qualified as a finalist in the solo competition.

But the strain had taken its toll. When she had completed her last performance, she returned to the hotel and fell, exhausted, into bed. At 6:30 the next morning she awoke to discover that not only had she and Augustyn been awarded first prize in the pas de deux, she had also won a silver medal in the solo competition.

Over the next few years both her repertoire and reputation continued to grow. Still at the outset of her career, she saw herself recognized as one of the few North American ballerinas to pose a threat to the stranglehold held so long over the ballet world by the Russians and Europeans.

It was a heady life for a woman in her 20s. Yet, the fame and attention did not make her overbearing. Free of the tempermental outbursts and egocentric demands that many top stars used as a tool, she was perhaps too malleable for her own good. The control she had held over her life during the early stages of her career had begun to weaken. More and more she found herself giving in to the demands of others.

Her only peace came from the time she spent away from the troupe. She bought a house in the renovated Cabbagetown area of Toronto and shared it with her brother, an intern at Toronto East General Hospital, and one of her sisters. As her schedule became more hectic, her privacy became a commodity to be closely guarded.

But even away from the rehearsal hall, her ability to lead a normal life was serverely limited. Fearing that any interest outside ballet would weaken her dedication, the only escape she allowed herself was the sedentary pleasure of enjoying her home.

Over the years, the time she had even to ensconce herself in Cabbagetown trickled down to a few weeks a year. Paris, London, Vienna, New York, Melbourne, Chicago — she danced in them all to dazzling acclaim. The more she travelled, the more widely she became known. But the constant exposure to strange surroundings continued to upset her just as much as it had when she first joined the National Ballet. In order to grow artistically, she had to meet all the demands and the pressure finally began to grow.

Not even her daily practice sessions could be allowed to lapse. Her performance depended upon her physical condition and she exercised faithfully. Gradually she noticed that her life had become an unending succession of exercises, classes, rehearsals and performances. The only way she could cope with it was to forget the future and concentrate totally on the present. Her goal was perfection and she was unwilling to settle for anything less.

Once, on a tour of Atlantic Canada, the troupe was trapped overnight by an October snowstorm. Unwilling to miss even one rehearsal, Karen and the other members of the National Ballet held their morning exercise class on the deck of a C.N. Ferry as they crossed the Northumberland Strait.

Yet, despite the intensity of her desire to excel, Karen still had the ability to laugh. On one occasion during a dress rehearsal of "The Sleeping Beauty" she decided to liven things up by giving Prince Charming something to think about. Switching her regular costume for a witch's wig, leotard, leg warmers and horn rimmed glasses, she lay down on her bed and waited for Frank Augustyn, her prince, to come and awaken her with a kiss. When he did, he gave a most unprincely snort and the whole troupe burst into laughter.

But such moments of relief were few and far between. Occasionally the physical and emotional demands of her career became so intense that she performed feeling tired and sick. During a brief holiday in Copenhagen she was tracked down by Rudolf Nureyev and asked to dance as his partner on a tour of Australia. Tired and homesick, Karen wanted to say no. But when Nureyev insisted, she gave in with the result that she performed badly and shattered her self-confidence.

By 1979 it had all become too much. She wanted to be a dancer, not a celebrity, and the pace was beyond her. In a moment of unguarded bitterness she said she thought she would have been better off and happier in musical comedy. When whispers began to circulate first that she had reached a plateau and then that she had entered a slump, she felt like her world had fallen in on top of her. Finally, in August, 1979 at London's Covent Garden, she touched bottom. Reviewers criticized her style and characterization and wrote her off as has-been.

Fed up and discouraged, Karen took a leave of absence from the National Ballet and went on an extended vacation. Giving up even her daily exercise classes, she allowed herself to drift. In the end she realized that if she wanted to continue dancing she would have to rework her career by placing the demands of ballet and her need for a personal life in a more even balance.

The process of picking up the pieces was long and arduous. Her professional reputation had suffered badly and it appeared her options in reestablishing it were limited. Finally, Roland Petit of the Ballet National de Marseille invited her to dance in his upcoming production of "Coppélia."

Alone in a studio in Marseille playing a videotaped version of "Coppélia" in which she had starred years before, Karen fought to recapture her old technical precision. Driving herself relentlessly, she made remarkable progress and in March, 1980 went on to give a creditable performance. Later that year she went with Petit to New York and danced to acclaim more glowing than ever.

For Karen the favourable reviews had a special significance. Not only did they mean she had recovered professionally, but they also proved that she had reestablished herself personally.

Gone were the days when she allowed herself to be manipulated. She had rediscovered the satisfaction of controlling her own life and of asserting a self-assurance that would help make her career work for her rather than against her.

Weekly visits to a psychiatrist helped her deal more reasonably with her desire to excel and also helped her put the demands of her career in clearer focus. She learned to leave the strain of training backstage and not to let it seep through into her personal life. Never an extrovert, she finally realized that beneath the strength of her dedication lay the fragility of her self-doubt.

After her triumph in New York with Petit, she returned to the National Ballet and opened the 1981 spring season in Toronto to enthusiastic reviews. In 1982 she made four guest appearances in Europe and performed the role of the Genie of the Ring in the 1982 British pantomime, "Aladdin and his Magic Lamp," at the Royal Alexandra Theatre in London.

In 1983 she expanded her life on several fronts. Early in the year she established a sense of permanence that had long been missing by marrying Canadian actor, Ross Petty. Later in the year she surprised her colleagues by signing a contract for her first book, *Karen Kain's Fitness and Beauty Book*. The project, which was an entirely new experience for her, took over a year to complete and is something Karen is especially proud of.

Something she is equally proud of is her performance in the National Ballet's three act production of "Don Quoxite." Starring once again with her former partner, Frank Augustyn, she has earned glowing reviews and thunderous applause — and that for Karen Kain is what life is all about.

L.M. MONTGOMERY

A gaunt old woman, her cheeks sunken and pale, stood shaking her finger in vexation at the scowling eight-year-old. "I've told you before, Maud, God frowns on reckless children who tear their clothes. Now you get down on the floor and pray for forgiveness for ripping that pinafore."

Maud Montgomery looked up at her grandmother darkly. No other girl her age had to pray on her knees in the middle of the kitchen every time she did something wrong and she was tired of it.

"Hurry up, Maud," her grandmother scolded, "before it's too late. God has no time for the stubborn and rebellious."

With a deep sigh of frustration, Maud sank to her knees. Her cheeks burned with anger and humiliation and after a few mumbled words of unfelt contrition, she scrambled to her feet and ran from the room.

"And don't you forget," her grandmother shouted after her, "the man from the Bible Society will be here in half an hour and I expect you to be on your best behaviour!"

Maud pounded up the stairs to her room and slammed the door behind her. If she had to kneel and pray once more today she knew she would scream. Why couldn't religion make her feel happy like it had when she was four and Aunt Emily had shown her where Heaven was? Maud sat down on her bed, drew her knees up under her chin and sighed wistfully. It had been such a perfect day. She and Aunt Emily had gone up to the attic of Clifton Presbyterian Church; why they had gone, Maud could never remember but it wasn't important. All that mattered was that she had asked Aunt Emily where Heaven was and Aunt Emily had pointed upwards to a square hole in the ceiling. It had made Maud feel safe and happy and had made her think that God was kind. But that had happened only once. When she was with her grandmother, God seemed different.

Half an hour later Maud, in a new pinafore, dragged herself downstairs for the semiannual visit of the traveller from the Bible Society. As she tiptoed into the living room, she saw him reading to her grandmother with his cadaverous face buried deeply in a Bible.

For what seemed like hours, Maud sat decorously in her chair staring at the floor, blotting out the traveller's voice by tracing pictures in the patterned carpet. Suddenly, just as she had spotted the profile of a withered witch, he leaned forward, grabbed her arm and squealed in an hysterical burst of zeal, "Little girl, isn't it nice to be a Christian?"

Maud stared at him in revulsion and hastily drew away her arm. His enraptured smile sickened her. She wanted desperately to tell him what she really felt — that if he was a Christian, she didn't want to be one — but she knew if she did she would spend the next three hours on the kitchen floor. Instead, she smiled and nodded. It was not the first time she had hidden her feelings behind a smile and it would certainly not be the last.

Lucy Maud Montgomery was born in Clifton (now New London), Prince Edward Island on November 30, 1874. When she was twenty-one months old her mother, Clara, died and her father, Hugh Montgomery, a country merchant, gave custody of her to her maternal grandparents, Alexander and Lucy Macneill.

Although she had many relatives on nearby farms, Maud (as she preferred to be called) spent much of her early life alone. In the richness of her imagination she created two companions who lived in the glass doors of her grandmother's china cabinet. Katie, the girl in the left-hand door, did not like Lucy who lived to the right, but Maud got along with them both and refused to favour one over the other.

From her earliest days, Maud maintained that she remembered seeing her mother lying in her coffin. Certainly, the image of her dead mother was vividly etched in Maud's mind, but it is more likely the scene she recalled grew from stories she was told as a child and not from something she actually remembered. At family gatherings tales of the past were told with great regularity and Maud listened to them all with rapt attention.

In fact, the only thing she liked better than being told stories, was being taken for long romps in the out-of-doors. Running free through the fields and orchards of Prince Edward Island, she came to know and to cherish every nook and cranny of her grandfather's farm. The scenery around Cavendish was breathtaking and she developed a love of the countryside that remained with her the rest of her life. Frequent visits from her father completed her joy and until she was six, Maud was a happy, carefree child.

Then, in 1881, she went to school for the first time. Dressed in starched pinafores, which none of the other children wore, and forced to go home for lunch while her classmates nibbled out of intriguing lunch buckets, Maud felt like an outsider from the very first day. Adding to her woes was the strict Presbyterianism her grandparents had begun to impress upon her now that she was older. Constant prayers for forgiveness of her childish sins nettled Maud and a resentment of both her grandparents and organized religion began to take deep root. Although she was in many ways fond of her grandparents, she would never forget the inflexibility of their religious training.

A year after she started school, Maud saw her father off on what was the first of a long series of trips to Saskatchewan. Although she missed him at first, Maud soon focused her attention on Wellington and David Nelson, two small boys who had come to board with the Macneills in Cavendish. With her two new companions, she ran happily through the woods and fields, fishing, picking berries, planting gardens and building playhouses. The three became fast friends and the memory of the idyllic days they spent together remained with them all for years to come.

As she progressed in school and learned to read, Maud discovered a world of even greater richness than that of the fields and orchards. Although her grandparents lived in a provincial backwater, they were far from boorish and their bookshelves were stocked with the best of prose and poetry. Maud was enthralled with both the words and pictures of the carefully preserved volumes and with an omnivorous appetite she devoured them all.

Soon reading was not enough. At the age of nine, inspired by the Scottish poet, James Thomson, she decided to write poetry of her own. The results thrilled her and in school she began to compose on her slate when she should have been concentrating on arithmetic.

In the months that followed she made her first atempt to write a short story and before long her poems and stories had begun their rounds to unsuspecting publishers. As the rejection slips poured in, Maud felt the first bitter stab of discouragement. But her desire had been kindled and it would take more than a rejection slip to extinguish it.

In 1890 one of her stories, "The Wreck of the Marco Polo," placed third for Queen's County in the Canada Prize Competition. Her work was reviewed in the Charlottetown *Patriot* and three months later, with the thrill of her first triumph still coursing through her veins, she left for Prince Albert, Saskatchewan to live with her father who had remarried and taken up permanent residence there three years before.

When she first arrived in Prince Albert, Maud. was fascinated by her new surroundings and thrilled with both her new stepmother and half sister, Kate. Before long, however, the novelty wore off and she started to resent her stepmother for the place she had taken in Hugh Montgomery's affections. The situation grew even worse a few months later when her stepmother's second child was born and Maud found herself being used as a live-in baby sitter.

Longing for Cavendish, she sought solace in her writing. One day her thoughts turned to a story her grandfather had told her years before about murder and piracy in the early days of settlement on Prince Edward Island. The memory inspired Maud and she sent a thirty-nine verse poem on the subject to the Charlottetown *Patriot*. For weeks she heard nothing. Then, one night late in November, her father came home with a copy of the paper and there on the front page was Maud's first epic. Her joy knew no bounds — she had finally been published!

It was only the beginning. A few months later an essay

she had written on her impressions of Saskatchewan appeared in the Prince Albert *Times* and in the weeks that followed several of her stories and poems were published in a variety of magazines.

But not even the pleasure of seeing her work appear in print could dispel Maud's growing homesickness, and in the summer of 1891 she returned to Cavendish. From then until her father died eight years later, virtually her only contact with him was through a sporadic exchange of letters. As she grew older, the absence of a strong parental influence in her life deeply wounded her and she began to build a wall around herself that few would ever penetrate.

Shortly after her return to Prince Edward Island, she spent a year with relatives in Park Corner giving music lessons and writing poems for the Charlottetown *Patriot*. The following autumn she want back to Cavendish to prepare for the entrance examination to Prince of Wales College in Charlottetown. She passed the exam and in 1894, after a year of study, was awarded a Second Class Teaching Certificate and sent to teach in a small school in Bideford, near Cavendish. Although she was finally on her own, Maud soon discovered that she had chosen the wrong profession. The tedium of the classroom quickly palled on her and to provide an outlet for her frustration, she began to get up early in the morning and write until it was time to go to school.

The following autumn she entered Dalhousie University in Halifax and enrolled in a special course in literature. The experience stimulated and inspired her and when, during her time in Halifax, she began to receive cheques from a variety of publications for her stories and poems, her joy knew no bounds. The more she wrote, the more she wanted to write something really worthwhile. But she didn't earn enough from her stories to support herself financially and with a grim sense of resolution, she realized she would have to return to the classroom.

In July, 1895 she received her First Class Teaching License and was assigned to a school first in Belmont and then in Lower Bedeque. When her grandfather died in 1898, she resigned her position and went back to Cavendish to live with her grandmother. With the exception of a brief respite in

82

Halifax during the fall of 1901 and spring of 1902, she remained there for the next thirteen years.

The few short months she spent away from Prince Edward Island working for the *Daily Echo* (the evening edition of the *Halifax Chronicle*) were among the happiest of her life. Proof-reading, editing the society page, writing columns — she did it all, and in what little spare time she had, she continued writing and selling articles of her own. But nothing she had written had yet to satisfy her. Poetry meant more to her than prose ever could and she longed — even though she knew she did not have the talent — to write something that would make her the equal of Byron or Tennyson.

As months flew by, her list of credits continued to grow and although much of her writing was contrived and mawkish, her cheques became larger and more frequent.

In June, 1902 she reluctantly left the paper and returned to Cavendish to resume her role as housekeeper to her lonely and ageing grandmother. Suddenly life had lost its glow. As a woman of twenty-eight, she found herself moldering away in the middle of nowhere.

The only thing in life that meant anything to her was her writing and she struggled feverishly to create something she could be truly satisfied with. But as the years went by, she continued to turn out the same mediocre stories she had in the beginning and the frustration, combined with the barrenness of her life in Cavendish, started to take its toll. Nervous spells and sick headaches began to plague her and for days at a time she was confined to her room.

Only in the woods and fields could she feel hope and freedom and she found herself spending more and more time wandering alone in the out-of-doors. When her escape route was shut off and she had no alternative but to mingle with society, she drew a mask over her face so no one could guess how unhappy she really was.

Thus, to the people of Cavendish, Maud Montgomery was a gregarious young woman who enjoyed taking part in community activities. Not even her relatives suspected that deep down, beyond the smiles and laughter, was a woman trapped and lonely. Adding to her burden was the fact the religious training imposed upon her as a child had had an effect other that that which her grandparents had intended. Instead of a devout Christian, Maud discovered that she had grown up to be a confirmed skeptic. To keep up appearances, she taught Sunday School and went to church, but it was a torment to her. She abhorred communal prayer and could not accept the divinity of Christ.

Gradually she began to develop an interest in mental telepathy and reincarnation. She found a comfort in the thought of transmigration of souls that was missing in conventional Christian tenets and as the years passed, she put increasing importance on premonitions and presentiments and on the possibility of reincarnation.

In what brief moments she had to devote to her writing, she tried to escape the confines of her own life by creating far away worlds of her own. Eventually she decided that short stories were not enough and in 1904 she started work on a book. The entire plot was worked around a brief entry she had scribbled in a notebook years before: "Elderly couple apply to orphan asylum for a boy. By mistake a girl is sent to them."

When the novel was finished in the fall of 1905, she sent it off to five publishers and promptly recieved five curt rejection slips. After the fifth rejection, she took the manuscript and tossed it in a closet.

A year passed. Then, rummaging through the same closet in the fall of 1906, she discovered the dogeared pages and set to work revising them. In the spring of 1907, with her hopes higher than they had ever been, she sent the new draft off to L.C. Page and Company of Boston.

Two months later a letter came in the mail accepting the book and offering her the choice of a lump sum payment or a ten per cent royalty. Preferring the idea of having her income spread over a number of years, Maud chose the royalty and late in the spring of 1908 *Anne of Green Gables* made its first appearance.

Although Maud had, at Page's request, immediately begun work on a sequel, she was under no illusions about the merit of her work. Anne's success flabbergasted her. In five months it had gone through six editions. The reviews were excellent and by May, 1914 the book, which would eventually be translated into more than fifteen languages, was in its thirty-eighth printing.

There was only one cloud on Maud's horizon. She had hoped the reviews would point out flaws and so help her improve her style. But there was no agreement. What one critic condemned another praised and she found it too confusing to draw conclusions.

At first the whirl of recognition that followed the publication of *Anne of Green Gables* dazzled Maud, but when the demands of publicity started to invade her private life, she drew the line. Sick headaches once again began to plague her and she retreated into herself. She finished *Anne of Avonlea* in November, 1908 and then went back to writing poems and short stories.

The second Anne book was a letdown to Maud and she felt that if it sold well she would be pressured into turning out a whole series of books at the expense of more serious writing. Within months her fears were realized. Her public and publishers quickly clamoured for more and over the next thirty years she added six new books to the series. The sequels, which were not written in strict chronological sequence of the heroine's life, took Anne through college, a career, marriage, motherhood and middle age.

In 1910 Maud created a new heroine and started to write her third book, *The Story Girl*. Before the book was published in May, 1911 it had become Maud's favourite. She felt it was more literary than anything she had ever written and she hoped it would point the way to greater artistic development.

Meanwhile, two months before *The Story Girl* appeared in print, Mrs. Macneill had died at the age of eighty-five. The loss created a vacuum in Maud's life and for several months she lived with relatives in Park Corner. Then, in the spring, she made the startling announcement that she had been secretly engaged for five years and would marry Ewan Macdonald, a Presbyterian minister four years her senior, on the fifth of July.

At the time of the engagement in 1906, Maud and Macdonald had decided to postpone the wedding until after Mrs. Macneill's death. Ostensibly, Maud did not want to create an upheaval for her grandmother. But there may have been other reasons as well.

Before she was introduced to Macdonald, Maud had met an attractive and successful man to whom she was immediately drawn. Mistaking her feelings for love, she had become engaged to him, only to discover that in reality she loathed him. For a year she tried to force herself to believe that she still wanted to marry him, but in the end she realized it was pointless and broke off the engagement. Once she was free, she found that she was suddenly very fond of him, but she knew her feelings could never blossom into love and she finally stopped seeing him altogether.

A short time later she fell in love with a man whom she later described as unattractive, unintelligent, and uninspired. Although she realized that marrying him would be a disaster, her physical attraction to him was so strong that she was only prevented from going through with the wedding by his unexpected death.

By the time Ewan Macdonald came into her life, Maud was looking for someone who could offer a relationship midway between the two she had already experienced. With his good looks, undemanding nature, and established position, Ewan seemed to be exactly what she needed. He aroused neither her love nor her loathing and she felt much more secure in basing her marriage on reason rather than emotion.

After a wedding trip to the British Isles, Maud and her new husband moved to Leaksdale, Ontario where Ewan had been appointed pastor of the Presbyterian Church. The congregation warmed to Maud and she soon settled into a new and demanding way of life. Although she took part in committees and social activities and performed all the duties expected of her as a minister's wife, she found the invasion of her privacy difficult to cope with.

The time she had to devote to her writing quickly diminished and when in 1912 at the age of thirty-eight she became a mother for the first time, it appeared as though she would have to give up her career entirely. Three years later a second son was born and she found herself irretrievably tied to a life of domesticity.

The only way she could survive as a writer was to create time where none had previously existed. By getting up early in the morning and writing before the rest of the household was astir, she began to reassert herself professionally. But mounting pressure in her personal life made concentration difficult. It had gradually become clear to her that Ewan was not well. Bouts of insomnia and depression, which had been rare during the early days of their marriage, had begun to occur with increasing frequency and life in the manse had become extremely trying.

Occasional vacation trips to Prince Edward Island buoyed Maud's spirits, but there seemed always to be something waiting for her at home to wear her down. The hours spent smiling before the members of the congregation, listening to them voice beliefs she could never share, were a source of great aggravation to her. Only by hiding behind her mask could she maintain her composure and conceal from the world her unorthodox views.

By 1919 Ewan's health had begun to deteriorate rapidly. His depressions became deeper and darker and as they worsened, Maud clung more tenaciously than ever to the one hour she had in the morning to devote to her writing. Between 1921 and 1931 she turned out scores of stories and poems and completed seven full-length books. Only one of these novels, *Emily of New Moon* really satisfied her. Although she denied suggestions that she had based Anne on herself, she did admit that in some respects Emily and Maud were one.

In 1926 Ewan was appointed pastor of the Presbyterian Church in Norval, Ontario and despite the upheaval of moving, Maud continued with her writing. Late that summer, *The Blue Castle*, her first book directly aimed at an adult audience, was published by Frederick Stokes and Company of New York.

As the years passed, Maud threw herself more and more into her writing. Only by creating worlds of her own could she escape the disillusionment and frustration of her domestic life and rediscover the warmth and happiness of the fleeting preschool days she had known in Cavendish. Her books continued to sell as quickly as they were published and her readership grew with each passing month.

In February, 1931 *A Tangled Web*, her second and final book for adults, was published by Frederick Stokes and

Company. It did not live up to the expectations Maud had had when she first started working on it and as she finally accepted her limitations, she began to feel that she would never achieve her dream of writing something truly great.

The prospects dimmed even more in 1934 when Ewan suffered a complete breakdown and spent four months in a sanitarium. The long months of recuperation that followed at home wore Maud down and later in the year, at the age of sixty, she suffered a breakdown of her own.

In 1938 she wrote her last complete book, *Anne of Ingleside*, then went to Prince Edward Island for a long overdue rest. The outbreak of World War II in 1939 combined with Ewan's feeble mental state to undo all the good the trip had done and in 1940 she suffered a second and more severe breakdown.

She had long dreaded the thought of dying slowly and had once written that she hoped her death would come suddenly and without warning. But it was not to be. All through the early years of the war she saw her life ebb slowly away. Gone were the hopes of writing a classic novel. There was nothing left to cling to and on April 24, 1942 she died at the age of sixty-seven.

Although she had failed to realize her dream of becoming a critical success, she had experienced the satisfaction of knowing that her work was at the very least a popular success. In the years since her death her novels have continued to sell at an astonishing rate and since 1954 more than seven million copies have been sold in Japan alone. Shadows of her life and of the people she knew endure in her work and the soul of Anne, so lovingly created, lives on in everyone who cherishes the memory of carefree childhood.

MAZO DE LA ROCHE

The drapes were drawn against the grey November dusk and in the rosy glow of firelight, the drawing room was transformed into a warm, protective womb.

Two girls — one fair and frail, the other dark and vibrant — sat cross-legged on the carpet staring into the flickering flames.

"If it's pretend, I can do it," Caroline said determindedly as she stroked her fingers through her long blonde hair. "But I think first you'll have to show me how."

"Show? There's nothing to show," Mazo huffed contemptuously. "You just think it and do it." Gingerly she picked up a cinder that had fallen on the carpet and tossed it back into the fireplace. "It's like the time I had a dream and woke up feeling that I'd been in a whole new world. All I have to do to make the feeling come back is pretend I'm someone different."

Caroline looked at her dubiously.

"You don't believe me? Well, I'll show you!" Mazo hunched forward and squeezed shut her eyes. "My name is Lautrec and I'm a captain with the French Foreign Legion. You can be Farah, an Arabian princess, and I'll come and rescue you from murderous tribesmen." She squinted warily at Caroline out of her left eye. "Just believe you're the princess and say what she'd say when I come to save you."

"All right," Caroline sighed, "but if I don't do it properly remember it's only my first time."

Mazo screwed up her face in a ferocious scowl and held high her hand to summon her troops. "To arms! To arms! The fair Farah awaits!" She jolted away across the scorching desert in search of the nomad camp. After a bloody duel with the Arab chieftain she swept up Farah, who sobbed out her thanks, and whisked her back to the legion barracks.

When they had finished their game, the two girls lay back on the carpet and roared in delight.

"Oh, Mazo, it's wonderful! It's better than a book — you can live it yourself."

"Better than a *book?* It's better than anything! And if you keep it a secret, we can do it again. We can make up new people and think up new stories and go anywhere in the world whenever we please!"

Mazo Roche was born in Toronto, Ontario on January 15, 1879. As the only child of William Roche, a moderately successful commercial traveler, and his wife, Alberta, she expected to be, and often was, the center of attention. Her parents doted on her and were determined to make her childhood one long succession of happy memories.

But it was not always an easy task. William changed jobs with great regularity and during his married life he moved his family a total of seventeen times. The frequent upheavals were unsettling for Mazo. Yet it appeared they could not be helped. With their great fondness for comfortable living, William and Alberta were constantly in search of the perfect house; nothing satisfied them for long and when they tired of one place, they simply moved on to the next.

As she grew older, Mazo gradually adjusted to her nomadic existence. With her burgeoning imagination as her sole companion, she began to create a fantasy world of her own, reliving the past and visualizing the future. Her pastime assumed even greater dimensions when, at the age of seven, she met her cousin, Caroline Clement for the first time. The two became fast friends and soon shared each other's innermost secrets. Caroline was intrigued by Mazo's ability to create imaginary characters and they began to act out scenes in which they played the parts of make-believe heroes.

Not long after their first meeting, the two girls began to dabble in writing and a tiny newsletter, printed by hand and sold to members of the family, began its brief existence. This fleeting journalistic venture instilled in Mazo a desire to continue with her writing.

A year and a half later, at the age of nine, she entered a

short story competition for children sixteen and under. Carried away by what she considered the beauty of her prose, she saw no reason why she should not be the winner. When the envelope returning her unrewarded manuscript finally arrived, she was devastated. Not even the editor's comment that her work showed remarkable promise could cheer her. In her own eyes she was a failure.

For a long time after that she refused to write anything. Instead, she devoted herself to the lessons she and Caroline received at a small private day school run by an Irishwoman. Mazo's aptitude for reading placed her well beyond her age group and after devouring the childhood classics, she moved on at the age of ten to tackle books by Charles Dickens.

Then, in 1890 Mazo and Caroline suffered a wrenching separation. Alberta Roche had been plagued by ill health for several years and her doctor felt the drier air of Galt would speed her recovery. Expecting their stay to be relatively brief, the Roches took a suite of rooms at a fashionable hotel.

For Mazo, life without Caroline was flat and flavourless. But as time passed, she became caught up in the excitement of hotel living and soon settled into her new surroundings. The comings and goings fascinated her and with her imagination working at fever pitch, she invented a variety of fates for the unsuspecting guests.

During the long winter evenings her pastimes were more conventional. Nestling down in her father's lap, she listened as he wiled away the hours by reading to her from her favourite books. A closeness developed between them that would last until William's death and Mazo began to look upon him as her hero and companion.

The second year of their stay in Galt did not pass as pleasantly. Alberta's health showed no improvement and as William began to spend long weeks away on business, Mazo experienced an increasing sense of doom. With her probing intellect and fecund imagination she became preoccupied with the strangeness of life and the possibility of death. A feeling of helplessness took possession of her and she feared being left alone.

As their last year in Galt drew to a close, the Roches realized that Alberta's health had deteriorated. Tired of hotel living, they decided to return to Toronto and live for a time with Alberta's parents.

For Mazo it was a welcome change. Gone were the lonely hours she had spent by herself while her mother rested. In their place came the warmth and security of life in a large family — a family which included not only Mazo, her parents and maternal grandparents, bu also an aunt and two uncles. Before long Caroline came to join them.

The two girls quickly resumed their games of make-believe and added new characters to their established cast. Drawing on situations from the plays they saw during frequent trips to the theater, they soon had a large and varied repertoire. Every hour they could spare was spent indulging their imaginations.

As time passed and Mazo grew from childhood to adolescence, Mrs. Roche's health improved and the pall of doom that had hovered over Mazo since her years in Galt, gradually disappeared. The bold aggressiveness of early childhood reasserted itself and she took up drawing and music and attended school at Parkdale Collegiate Institute.

Yet, despite her new interests, she continued to favor Caroline's shy and retiring company above all else. The differences in their makeup seemed to draw them closer to each other and the one trait they had in common — their great sensitivity — made the bond complete. A harsh word, a sidelong glance and both would burst into bitter tears.

In 1900 the comfort of a secure homelife came to a sudden end when Mazo's grandfather died and her grandmother sold the family house. Once again Mazo (then twenty-one) and her parents resumed their wandering rounds. A year or two in one house and they moved on to something different. But this time, at least, Mazo had the comfort of knowing that Caroline would make the tedious rounds with them.

Taking the upheavals in stride, Mazo continued with her sketching and finally enrolled in the Ontario School of Art. Her drawing showed promise and she vaguely thought of becoming a professional book illustrator. During this unsettled period she made her first serious attempt at writing a short story.

Using the surname "de la Roche" and writing in secret so no one would know if her manuscript was rejected, she gave free rein to her imagination. When the story was finished, she sent it off to *Munsey's Magazine* and began a long vigil waiting for a reply.

Weeks passed. Finally, a small envelope came in the mail enclosing a letter of acceptance and a cheque for $50. Mazo was thrilled. More stories followed in rapid succession and most were accepted for publication.

As her credits grew, she began to take increasing pains with her work, revising and recopying manuscripts until the results completely satisfied her. In 1903 she wrote what she considered her best story to date and sent it off, full of confidence.

As time passed and she received no reply, she grew increasingly fretful. Her health deteriorated and she could no longer concentrate. When it finally became obvious that she would not hear back, she grew obsessed by a feeling of failure and soon suffered a nervous breakdown. During the long months of recuperation she was too weak even to read a book. Gradually, however, her strength returned and later in the year she returned to her writing.

Life resumed its normal course and for several years the Roches remained in Toronto. Then, in 1910 William made a sudden and startling decision. He was tired of urban living and wanted to buy a farm. Lack of agricultural experience did not deter him and when he heard of a suitable property for sale between Toronto and Hamilton, he quickly bought it.

From the very beginning, the venture was a comedy of errors. Only William's efforts to redecorate the house bore satisfactory results. Each member of the family concentrated on a different area of expertise, all with equally bleak results. Mazo chose Leghorn hens and in the time she had left from doing her chores and helping with the house, she continued with her writing. Often the strain was too much. But she persisted and eventually broke into the lucrative American market.

It was during this time that Mazo fell in love with Pierre Mansbendel, a civil engineer she had met at a rooming house owned by her widow aunt, Eva Smith. Handsome, serious and highly sensitive, Pierre was everything Mazo had ever wanted in a man and his devotion to her only served to heighten her passion.

Yet the ardour of her feelings disturbed Mazo — with her thoughts wrapped up in Pierre, she had little time to devote to her writing. When he finally announced that he wanted to visit the farm and meet her parents, Mazo's feelings were mixed.

They grew even more confused when she discovered that Pierre wanted to spend his time alone, with her, taking long walks in the fields and flying kites. She enjoyed being with him but she needed time to herself and she quickly realized that if she were ever to be happy in a relationship with a man, he would have to give her the freedom to pursue her own life. In her mind, Pierre was not prepared to do it and from that time on she found no tranquility in his companionship.

The tension was relieved when Aunt Eva arrived for an unexpected visit. A keen judge of human nature, she quickly sensed Mazo's unease and joined Pierre in his trips to the fields. For Mazo it offered time to collect her thoughts and she came to the conclusion that more than anything else — more even than being with the man she loved — she wanted to be alone, at work on her writing. But it was not that simple. Time after time she sat down at her desk only to find herself still distracted by thoughts of Pierre.

When the visit finally came to an end, Pierre returned to Toronto and rented the entire top floor of Eva's house. He and Mazo continued to see each other, but they were both content to let their relationship drift.

Gradually they realized they would never marry. Mazo's writing meant too much to her and she was too wrapped up in helping — vainly — to keep the farm on an even keel. In May, 1914 Pierre quietly married Aunt Eva. She was fifty-eight, he thirty-eight. For Mazo, then thirty-five, the news was bittersweet. Her greatest consolation was the fact the newlyweds had packed up their belongings and moved to New York.

A few weeks after the unexpected wedding announcement, Mazo wrote a short story and sent it off to the *Atlantic Monthly*, one of the most prestigious magazines then in publication in the United States. Its acceptance was a major accomplishment for her, but before she had the satisfaction of seeing it in print, her father died and her world fell apart.

In the long months that followed, Mrs. Roche decided that Mazo and Caroline should accompany her back to Toronto. She sold the farm and once again the tiny family was on the move. This time, however, the Roche's financial situation was extremely poor. Without William's income to fall back on, the future looked bleak. To help ease the situation, Caroline went to work for the Civil Service and Mazo began to turn out stories with increased regularity.

Five years passd uneventfully. Then, in 1920, Mrs. Roche died and Mazo and Caroline, facing a major crossroad in their lives, decided to spend the summer apart to consider the future.

Mazo unwisely went to New York to visit Eva and Pierre. From the moment she arrived, the situation was untenable. On the few occasions she was left alone with Pierre, she experienced a mixed feeling of embarrassment and guilt and felt as though Eva was watching her every move. The days dragged on in an endless succession of stress and pretense and when the time finally came for her to board the train for the long journey home, she breathed a sigh of relief.

Once reunited with Caroline, she set to work on a series of one act plays and entered her favourite in two competitions — one sponsored by the I.O.D.E. and the other by the Author's Association of Montreal. When the results were announced, Mazo found that she had been awarded first prize in both competitions. Her confidence soared. Her work began to attract critical interest and in 1922 *Explorers of the Dawn*, a collection of short stories (some previously published in magazines), was published by the Alfred A. Knopf Company of New York. The reviews were enthusiastic and within weeks the book appeared on American best seller lists.

Explorers of the Dawn was followed a year later by Mazo's first novel, *Possession*, which also became an immediate hit. Spurred by her new found success, Mazo threw herself into her second novel, *The Thunder of New Wings*. Her star was ascending and at the age of forty-four, she wanted to make the most of it.

However, in her overeagerness, the new book fell short and Macmillan and Company of New York, publishers of *Possession*, refused to touch it unless it was completely rewritten. Deflated, Mazo tossed the manuscript aside. When the stab of rejection had finally lost its sting, she went to work on an entirely new novel and entitled it *Delight*. This time she met Macmillan's standards and after its publication in 1926, the new book went on to garner great critical praise in both England and the United States. Only in Canada was it denounced as a failure.

The favourable reviews thrilled Mazo. But not even their flattering phrases could make up for the feeling of devastation she experienced every time she read those that were unkind. The diatribe heaped upon *Delight* by Canadian critics chafed her for months. For a time she alternated between the desire to give up writing altogether and the desire to write a novel that would defy abuse. In the end, she rummaged through her desk and pulled out the closely written pages of *Jalna*, a half forgotten novel she had started in the summer of 1925.

Set in Ontario, the new book traced the lives and loves of the descendants of Philip Whiteoak. a wealthy British military officer who had carved his own empire out of the Ontario wilderness. Although rumours later circulated to the contrary, Jalna, the family home, was not based on any house Mazo had ever seen and the Whiteoaks bore no resemblance to any family other than Mazo's own.

When the manuscript was finished, Mazo sent it off to Macmillan who agreed to publish it in the very near future. Then as production got underway, Mazo read of a competition being held by the *Atlantic Monthly* for the most interesting novel by any author from any part of the world. The $10,000 prize tempted her and although *Jalna* had already been accepted, she decided to enter a carbon copy just to see what the judges would say.

As the weeks passed she began to worry about the duplicity she had shown in submitting a manuscript already scheduled for publication. When a letter came from Macmillan mentioning the correcting of proofs, she wrote to the *Atlantic Monthly* and asked the editor to return her submission. Politely, he declined. *Jalna* was one of three books being held for further consideration.

Immediately after she received the news, Mazo wrote to Macmillan, confessed her sin and asked that if she won they would release her from her contract. Incredibly enough, they agreed. Weeks dragged on and the suspense mounted. Finally, in April, 1927 a letter arrived announcing that *Jalna* had won the $10,000 prize and would be published in collaboration with Little, Brown and Company of Boston.

As news of the award leaked out, Mazo was deluged with demands for interviews and photo sessions. She thrived on the attention and felt more alive than she had for years. When the book was published on the seventh of October it became an immediate best seller. The first edition of 45,000 sold out within three days and by the end of the year, she had earned $50,000 in royalties.

It seemed too good to be true. But Mazo was determined to rise to even greater heights and plans for *Whiteoaks*, the sequel to *Jalna* had already begun to form in her mind. However, before she could write more than a few chapters, she suffered a nervous collapse that required long months of recuperation. As her strength gradually returned, she threw herself back into her work and saw the characters assume a dimension that, to Mazo at least, made them seem almost alive.

In 1929, after a trip to Europe, Mazo and Caroline settled in England. More books in the Whiteoak series followed and in 1936 a play, written by Mazo and based on her novels *Jalna* and *Whiteoaks*, opened in London for a hugely successful three year run.

Meanwhile, in 1931, Mazo and Caroline had adopted two children — a girl two and a half and a boy thirteen months — who had been left scantily provided for when their parents (friends Mazo and Caroline had made in Italy in 1929) died within six months of each other. The presence of children in their lives rejuvenated Mazo and Caroline and flooded them with memories of the carefree days they had shared years before. They were content and secure and happy to finally be able to put down roots.

Then, early in 1939, with the threat of war looming ever

more ominously, Mazo decided it would be safer to move her little family back to Canada. From that time on, her life lost its luster. She withdrew into her own world and devoted herself entirely to her work. Of the sixteen Whiteoak novels, ten were written after her return to Canada. The quality of the later books deteriorated noticeably and although sales remained brisk, Mazo was unable to recapture the power she had shown in *Jalna* and *Whiteoaks*. From time to time she ventured into other areas of writing, dabbling with varying success in children's stories and nonfiction.

In 1943 a long series of illnesses began that would plague her for the rest of her life. To make matters worse, the wartime economy affected the size of her royalty cheques and severely reduced her main source of income. The fifties brought in their wake disappointments with the children and it seemed to Mazo as though the only constants in her life were Caroline and her writing.

Her last years were spent quietly in Toronto where, despite her failing health, she continued to work, finishing her last book, *Morning at Jalna* in 1960. Although her novels were often compared unfavourably with those of John Galsworthy, they quickly became a hallmark of Canadian literature. Their popularity satisfied Mazo, not only because of the financial rewards it brought, but also because it nulified what she considered the shabby treatment her work had received at the hands of Canadian critics. She died on July 12, 1961 at the age of 82 and was buried near Lake Simcoe in the very heart of Whiteoak country.

BARBARA ANN SCOTT

Snowflakes were falling softly and gently and from the big picture window six-year-old Barbara Ann could see children sledding and skating on the Rideau River. Suddenly, from the far bank, a girl dressed in green spun across the ice in a figure eight. Barbara Ann pressed her nose against the frosty glass and watched in delight as the girl completed the loop.

It looked like such fun. All the laughter and play. All the dipping and whirling. More than anything else Barbara Ann wanted to be out on the river with skates of her own. Not ugly double blades that buckled over her boots like the pair her mother had given her when she was three. But real skates with white boots and silver blades — just like the ones Sonja Henie wore. She didn't care if it was cold on the river or if she fell twenty times a day. All she wanted was to spin and twirl and listen to her blades as they swished across the ice.

Hastily she wiped away the condensation her breath had left on the window. The girl in green had left the ice and was sitting on the bench taking off her figure skates. How Barbara Ann envied her! Every year for as long as she could remember she had written to Santa Claus asking for a pair of skates and a horse. So far all he'd managed to give her was the ugly old double blades.

Turning from the window, Barbara Ann held out her arms at right angles to her body and pretended to glide across the carpet. But it didn't work. Slippers weren't skates and carpets weren't rinks. There was only one answer and that was to write again to Santa Claus and tell him that if Sonja Henie had been given skates when she was a little girl, there was no reason why Barbara Ann Scott couldn't have them while she was still little.

With a sigh of determination, she turned back to the window and watched the river until the thickening snow blocked out the view.

Barbara Ann Scott was born in Ottawa, Ontario in 1929. Her father was a colonel and military secretary in the Department of Defense and Barbara Ann adored him. His pet name for her was "Tinker" and with a true sense of military precision he liked to see her neat and tidy and properly dressed. Above all, he wanted her to keep her fine blonde hair short and for a time Barbara Ann complied with his wishes. Then, as she grew older, she began to have second thoughts. Her friends started wearing curls and ringlets and they laughed at Barbara Ann because her straight hair made her look like a boy. Barbara Ann's mother soon rectified the situation by giving her pink silk ribbons to tie in her hair.

Always small for her age, Barbara Ann was closely guarded by her parents. As a baby she had suffered from severe mastoid inflammation and by the time she was three had undergone eight operations. Because of this, Mr. and Mrs. Scott were reluctant to see her take up skating.

Finally, when the problem had been corrected, they gave in and when Barbara Ann was six she received her first pair of figure skates. From the moment she opened the box, Barbara Ann wanted nothing more than to be taken to the Rideau River and taught how to skate. Unfortunately, she had a cold and wasn't allowed out of the house. Her parents offered a compromise and she wore the skates to bed.

That winter Barbara Ann started to take lessons at the Minto Skating Club in Ottawa. Her mother picked her up after school, drove her to the rink and waited while Barbara Ann had her lesson. From the very beginning it was obvious to her coaches that Barbara Ann had special talent. Her daintiness and grace promised great things ahead, but for the first few months Barbara Ann was not sure she wanted to spend all her free time skating.

She loved animals and liked to spend her after school hours looking after her cat, dog, rabbit, turtle and white rat. She also enjoyed playing with her dolls — especially a Charlie MacCarthy doll that had come dressed in top hat and tails.

100

Once, when Barbara Ann complained that Charlie was dressed for nighttime and not for daytime her father had his tailor make a doll-size suit and Mrs. Scott knit a wardrobe of sweaters.

But more than even playing with her pets and dolls, Barbara Ann liked being at home. She loved to help her mother get dinner ready on the cook's night off and as a little girl she said that what she wanted most out of life was to be a wife and have a home of her own. Skating was something she then did for fun and she did not take it very seriously.

In the winter of 1936 she went back to the Minto Skating Club for the second year and did what she was told and nothing more. When the time came to take her first test, her form was poor and she consequently failed. The news did not please Mr. Scott. Taking Barbara Ann on his knee, he told her that he never wanted to see her do anything halfheartedly again. If she wanted to skate she would have to apply herself and if she didn't, she should stop wasting her coach's time.

Barbara Ann took the words to heart and the following year, at the age of eight, passed her bronze test. After that her enthusiasm grew and she spent the summer at a skating school in Lake Placid, New York. The exposure to professional skaters and top ranked amateurs impressed her deeply and that winter she increased her practice time and passed the silver test.

Many other students at the Minto Skating Club resented the speed with which Barbara Ann was progressing. It had taken some of them years to pass even the bronze test and seeing a girl of nine with the silver behind her did not sit well with them. Often they got in her way as she spun figure eights and many times they knocked her down. But Barbara Ann did not give in. Brushing off the snow, she got back on her feet and resumed her practice.

In 1939, at the age of ten, Barbara Ann made a major sensation in the figure skating world by becoming the youngest person ever to pass the gold test. With each passing achievement she spent more time on the ice and when she was eleven she won the Canadian Junior Championship, which automatically put her in the senior division where she would have to compete with skaters eighteen and nineteen.

But Barbara Ann had confidence. A visit she had had

with the international figure skating sensation, Sonja Henie had instilled in her a sense of her own ability and a desire to achieve all she could. The visit with Sonja had come as a surprise. A major ice show had visited Ottawa shortly after Barbara Ann passed her gold test. Hearing of Barbara Ann's accomplishment, Sonja (who was starring in the show) invited her to tea and talked about skating. The magic of that visit had done more to firm Barbara Ann's determination to go as far as she could than all the medals and awards ever would.

After the Canadian Junior Championships Barbara Ann's parents took her out of school and she began to spend eight and nine hours a day at the Minto Skating Club. Her mother accompanied her to the rink and watched and knit as Barbara Ann trained. From October until April the routine was the same, with a private tutor taking up what few hours were left to keep Barbara Ann abreast of her schoolwork. In May and June she concentrated entirely on her studies and enjoyed the luxury of long weekends of play.

In 1942 Mr. Scott died and Barbara Ann experienced a deep sense of loss. For a time her skating suffered, but in the end she went back to it with her former enthusiasm. Two years later, when she was fifteen, she won the Canadian senior women's figure skating championship, then went on to capture the North American title. The first taste of major victory electrified her and made her a fierce competitor. Her desire to win was only equalled by her love of skating and with her innate ability and surging confidence, she was a power to be reckoned with.

The future was bright. With a little more work she could become a world champion. But before she could plan that far ahead she would have to find a way to pay her expenses. Equipment, costumes, coaches and travel all cost money and after years of financing Barbara Ann's lessons, Mrs. Scott was at the end of her resources.

Finally a group of Mr. Scott's friends came forward and offered to cover Barbara Ann's expenses for the foreseeable future. With that problem out of the way, Barbara Ann went to work on her training program and successfully defended her Canadian and North American titles. In 1947 she made her first trip to Europe where, in rapid succession, she won both the Women's European Championship and the Women's World Championship.

Congratulatory telegrams poured in from all across Europe and North America and she returned to Canada to a hero's welcome. In Toronto she was honored with a ticker tape parade and in Ottawa she was presented with a canary-coloured Buick convertible. Before she had time to enjoy it, however, criticism arose that as an amateur she had no right accepting gifts. In the end, to protect her amateur standing, she bowed to the pressure and returned the car.

After a brief rest she resumed her training and began to plan her program for the following year. Not only did she want to defend her European and World titles, she also wanted to win the Olympic title at St. Mortiz. Her schedule was grueling. Nine hours a day, six days a week she worked in the arena at Schumacher, Ontario practicing the same moves over and over again. On December 16, 1947 she flew to London to undergo final preparations for the three championships which would be held all within one month.

In Europe her welcome was cool. Many critics were skeptical of her ability to defend her titles and one went so far as to say she was the weakest figure skater to win the world championship in many years. Barbara Ann took the criticism with equanimity. The news that she had been named Canada's outstanding female athlete of 1947 bolstered her confidence and by the time she moved on to Prague to participate in the European championship she was ready both physically and mentally.

On January 14, 1948, the first day of competition, she placed first in the compulsory figures in a field of nineteen and moved on the next day to the free skating. When her name was finally called, she skated onto the ice and as the opening bars of music filled the arena, began her program. Then, suddenly, for the first time in a major competition, the music stopped. Not knowing whether to continue, stop or leave the ice, she decided the best course was to stand motionless. Within seconds the malfunction was corrected and she resumed her performance. The crowd roared its approval and moments later the judges declared her the winner.

As satisfying as the victory was, it was not the one she

was most interested in. World attention was focused on the Fifth Winter Olympic Games being held in St. Moritz and Barbara Ann was determined to capture the prestigious Olympic Crown. Competing against twenty-five champions from eleven countries, she maintained her poise and went on in the final competition to be placed first by eight of the nine judges.

A week later she won the World Championship and returned to Canada with the triple crown of women's international figure skating firmly in her possession. Her homecoming was even more tumultuous than it had been the year before and when the City of Ottawa again offered her a car, she unhesitatingly accepted: she had decided to turn professional and no longer had to worry about protecting her amateur standing.

Actually, the decision to turn professional had been an extremely difficult one for her to make. She thrived on the challenge of amateur competition but with the three major championships already to her credit, there was nothing left to strive for.

In the end, after lengthy discussions with her mother and friends of her father, she announced to the press that she had decided to turn professional and had established as her employer the St. Lawrence Foundation, a charitable organization she had formed to help crippled and underprivileged children. Under the terms of the foundation's charter, all her earnings were to go directly to the foundation and she was to receive an allowance, the size of which would depend on her need.

Late in 1948 the foundation received its first influx of working capital when Barbara Ann made her professional debut at the Roxy Theater in New York. Appearing on the same program with a host of variety acts and the film *That Wonderful Feeling* starring Tyrone Power, Barbara Ann skated an eight minute program from *Babes in Toyland*.

The next day Canadian newspapers from Halifax to Vancouver reported the debut in glowing reviews and announced that for the third year in a row, Barbara Ann had been named Canada's outstanding female athlete. But in New York the papers were silent. A week passed and not a word on

104

the debut was written. Then, on the thirtieth of December *Variety*, the show business weekly, finally acknowledged Barbara Ann's performance by saying: "Barbara Ann gets little chance to show off her more accomplished trick-skating routines due to the confinement of the ice area." It went on, however, to add: "The show is brightly costumed and built in a way that makes her an easy candidate for Hollywood." The entire $80,000 Barbara Ann received for her eight week engagement was handed directly over to the St. Lawrence Foundation.

Although she continued to enjoy skating, Barbara Ann soon found life as a professional far different from life as an amateur. Rehearsals and practices remained as stringent as ever, but the competitive edge she thrived on had disappeared. In its stead came the unrelenting pressures of show business. An entourage consisting of lawyers, an agent, publicity men and representatives to serve as escorts and advisers soon surrounded her and began organizing her life.

Makeup sessions, costume fittings and publicity appearances took up more time than ever before and at times Barbara Ann found the mounting pressure unbearable. Sometimes the attention she received when she went into a restaurant or department store made her feel like she was on display, while at other times the attention and kindness of strangers moved her to tears.

In 1950 she appeared in Canada's first major ice show, "Skating Sensations." Sellout audiences packed arenas all across the country and in 226 performances Barbara Ann and a cast of 56 travelled 12,000 miles, played to 850,000 fans and grossed more than $1,000,000.

In Stellarton, N.S. miners rushed to the stadium still wearing pit-lamps while in Saskatchewan a priest drove 350 miles through a snowstorm just to see the show. All across Canada the story was the same. Then, in Vancouver Barbara Ann came down with flu. She had no sooner recovered than she cracked two ribs during a performance in Calgary. After the show a doctor examined her and after taping her ribs found she had pleurisy and ordered her to bed for two weeks. Amid protests from Barbara Ann and her agent he relented and said if she had to skate she was not to do anything extra for at least two months.

Barbara Ann continued with the show and cancelled a scheduled appearence in a Calgary department store. The next day she went on to Edmonton where publicity men, unaware of her condition, had arranged for her to appear at a department store there. When they arrived, Mrs. Scott explained that it was impossible and suggested they drive by the store so Barbara Ann could wave at the crowds. Reluctantly the publicity men agreed.

Later that afternoon, Barbara Ann turned on the radio in her hotel room to hear an announcer criticize her for showing "such disregard for the happiness of children." The newspapers echoed the abuse and at a press conference held later that day to explain the situation, Barbara Ann received a cool reception.

The first performance in Edmonton was scheduled for the following evening and everyone associated with the show expected to skate to an empty house. Instead, the stadium was packed and at a free matinee held later in the week for children under ten, Barbara Ann received a huge ovation.

When the ice show completed its cross country tour, Barbara Ann had a brief rest then left for Los Angeles to spend a month as guest star with the U.S. Ice Capades. When her engagement ended she returned to Canada to spend what she hoped would be several peaceful weeks alone with her mother at a small summer cottage near Brockville, Ontario. Soon after their arrival, however, they began to receive letters and phone calls from a man saying that he had received Barbara Ann's message and that she was the only person in the world who could help him. One night, as Barbara Ann and her mother slept in an upstairs bedroom, a stranger began pounding on the door, demanding to see Barbara Ann. Mrs. Scott, who quickly realized it was the same man who had made the calls and written the letters, telephoned the police, then ran downstairs and shouted through the locked door that Barbara Ann wasn't there. A few moments later the police arrived and the man was taken into custody. Although she was shaken by the experience, Barbara Ann recognized it as an isolated incident and refused to dwell upon it.

In July her brief vacation came to an end and she flew to

England to make what was referred to in Canada as her theatrical debut at London's Harringay Arena. Before an audience of 8,000 she performed the title role of "Rose Marie on Ice," a skating spectacular based on the 1924 Friml-Hammerstein operetta "Rose Marie." The entire concept of an operetta on ice thrilled Barbara Ann, but she recognized her limitations and arranged for a professional actress to do the actual singing and talking before a concealed microphone while she mouthed the lyrics.

As the demands of her career grew, Barbara Ann the private citizen began to resent Barbara Ann the skating star. Unable to do many of the things she wanted to do in her personal life because of severe time restrictions, she nonetheless felt obligated to yield what little time she had to the demands of publicity men. She also perceived that the image which had been created for her — the image people believed was the real Barbara Ann — had little bearing on reality. At one point in her career she told a reporter that fans believed her to be something more than perfect and the whole idea frightened her.

By the time she was twenty-two, she had begun to regret the fact that since the age of nine she had not enjoyed an ordinary family life. The constant travel and rehearsals had become too much and she was tired of the artificiality of show business.

In the winter of 1950-51 she cleared her schedule and settled down with her mother in a small flat in Toronto. After thirteen years, the return to home life and its accompanying sense of normalcy and stability relaxed her and helped her realize what her priorities really were. She wanted to skate for a few more years, then retire from public view. Basically her dream was still the same one she had had years before in Ottawa — to marry and settle down in a home of her own.

As time passed and the glare of the spotlight gradually faded she saw her wish come true. After her marriage in 1956 she settled down to the life she had always wanted and today lives quietly with her husband in Chicago.

BIBLIOGRAPHY

Alspector, J.C. "Barbara Ann Scott," *Today*, February 20, 1981, p. 19.

Ayre, John. "The Reluctant Superstar," *Maclean's*, February 9, 1981, p. 43-48.

Carr, Emily. Growing Pains. Toronto: Oxford University Press, 1946.

- - - -. Hundreds and Thousands: The Journals of Emily Carr. Toronto: Clarke Irwin & Co. Ltd., 1966.

"Cold Cash," *Time*, May 8, 1950, p. 18-19.

Curzon, S.A. Laura Secord the Heroine of 1812. Toronto: C. Blackett Robinson, 1887.

Darling, Christopher. Kain & Augustyn. Toronto: The Macmillan Company of Canada, 1977.

de la Roche, Mazo, Ringing the Changes. London: Macmillan & Co. Ltd., 1957.

Dictionary of Canadian Biography Vol. IX. Toronto: University of Toronto Press, 1976. p. 405-407.

Edmonds, Alan. "Who Says You Can't Get a Ballerina off the Farm?," *Canadian Magazine*, February 15, 1975, p. 3-8.

Foster, Mrs. W. Garland. The Mohawk Princess. Vancouver: Lion's Gate Publishing Co., 1931.

Gillen, Mollie. The Wheel of Things: A Biography of L.M. Montgomery. Halifax: Formac Publishing Co. Ltd., 1983.

Hambleton, Ronald. Mazo de la Roche of Jalna. Toronto: General Publishing Co. Ltd., 1966.

Kostash, Myrna. Her Own Woman. Toronto: The Macmillan Company of Canada, 1975.

LaMarsh, Judy. Memoirs of a Bird in a Gilded Cage. Toronto: McClelland & Stewart Ltd., 1969.

"Little Girl on Ice," *Time*, July 24, 1950, p. 32-33.

Livingstone, David. "Karen Kain at 30," *Chatelaine*, May, 1981, p. 51.

MacDermot, H.E. Maude Abbott: A Memoir. Toronto: The Macmillan Company of Canada, 1941.

Maynard, Olga. "A Canadian Swan: The National Ballet's Karen Kain," *Dance Magazine*, June, 1974, p. 36-39.

McRaye, Walter. Pauline Johnson and her Friends. Toronto: The Ryerson Press, 1947.

Newman, Peter C. "Judy Leaves the Gilded Cage," *Maclean's*, November 10, 1980, p. 38.

Pearson, Carol. Emily Carr as I Knew Her. Toronto: Clarke, Irwin & Co. Ltd., 1954.

Pickford, Mary. Sunshine and Shadow. New York: Doubleday & Co. Inc., 1955.

Roxborough, Henry. Great Days in Canadian Sport. Toronto: The Ryerson Press, 1957.

Street, David. Karen Kain Lady of Dance. Toronto: McGraw-Hill Ryerson Ltd., 1978.

Timson, Judith. "Working on the Sequel," *Maclean's*, March 3, 1980, p. 8-10.

Tippett, Maria. *Emily Carr A Biography.* Toronto: Oxford University Press (Canada), 1979.

VanSteen, Marcus. *Pauline Johnson Her Life and Work.* Toronto: Musson Book Co., 1965.

Windeler, Robert. *Sweetheart The Story of Mary Pickford.* New York: Praeger Publishers, 1974.

Wuorio, Eva-Lis. "Backstage with Barbara Ann," *Maclean's,* February 15, 1949, p. 12-13, 48-49.

Zaslow, Morris (editor). *The Defended Border Upper Canada and the War of 1812.* Toronto: The Macmillan Company of Canada, 1964.